Sharing the Word

SALVATION
God's Greatest Miracle

Clay A. Kahler, Ph.D.

Wipf & Stock
PUBLISHERS
Eugene, Oregon

SALVATION: GOD'S GREATEST MIRACLE

Copyright © 2007 Clay A. Kahler. All rights reserved. Except for brief quotations in critical publications or reviews, no part of this book may be reproduced in any manner without prior written permission from the publisher. Write: Permissions, Wipf and Stock Publishers, 199 W. 8th Ave., Eugene, OR 97401.

ISBN 13: 978-1-55635-524-0

www.wipfandstock.com

Manufactured in the U.S.A.

ACKNOWLEDGEMENTS

There are many people to whom I owe a great debt. First to my many learned seminary professors who taught me well both inside the classroom and outside of it as well. These great men not only taught me Bible and Theology, but more importantly they taught me to think.

Dr. George Goolde
Dr. Gary Coombs
Dr. George Hare
Dr. David Myers
Dr. Garland Shin
Dr. Tony Crisp
Prof. Thomas Rohm

Then I owe the members and leaders of the First Baptist Church of Orrick MO. for their patience and their love. It is a privilege to serve as your pastor and I hope to continue until the Lord comes back.

Finally I want to thank my wife, Vicki S. Kahler for all of her help and encouragement.

Table of Contents

Introduction 7

Section 1 9

    Chapter 1 What Do You Mean You Hear God? 11

    Chapter 2 A Christ-Centered Relationship 21

    Chapter 3 One Who Was Close…Yet So Far Away 43

Section 2 Does God Grade on a Curve? 49

    Chapter 4 Remember the Curve 51

    Chapter 5 Why Doesn't God Grade on a Curve 59

    Chapter 6 Passing By the Grace of God 69

    Chapter 7 Living Beyond the Curve 81

Section 3 The Forgiveness of God 89

    Chapter 8 River of Forgiveness 91

    Chapter 9 Have We Been Too Bad To Be Forgiven? 95

    Chapter 10 Complete 105

    Chapter 11 Three Misbeliefs About Forgiveness 115

    Chapter 12 Biblical Examples of Forgiveness 129

Section 4 Our Justification by Faith 135

    Chapter 13 Who Needs To Know? 137

    Chapter 14 When the Guilty Go Free 141

    Chapter 15 One Substitution 153

    Chapter 16 Many Results 165

Selected Bibliography 175

Introduction

SALVATION

Approaching a subject as grand and awesome as Salvation is, to say the least, daunting. So, why take it on? Aren't there plenty of other good books on the subject? Yes there are, but at the same time, I am convinced that Salvation is a subject that can not be over explored. It is a subject that must be talked about over and over again. So, you may ask, what qualifies you to write about Salvation? Well, first and foremost, I have been saved. As such, I am a child of God... A joint-heir of Christ... I was once dead in my sins but now I am alive in Christ. Second, I am a " Fellow Elder" 1 Peter 5:1. I have been saved for the purpose of preaching Christ and Him crucified.

So, what is it that I am going to contribute to this discussion concerning grace, this miraculous work of salvation? Well, I hope to write to you from the perspective of a recipient of grace, rather than that of an academician. This Amazing Grace that we sing about is far too grand to disguise in scholasticism. It is in fact miraculous!

"In the beginning..." Oh how we love those words. They are not simply the opening words of Scripture, no; they are the welcome mat that leads one onto the presence of God. They also herald the second greatest miracle of all of Scripture, creation itself. From there we learn of Abram and the promise of a lineage even in his old age... We meet Moses and watch with baited breath as the Children of Israel cross the Red Sea. We learn of Joshua and see him gain supernatural victory after victory. We come a crossed Sampson, Gideon, Deborah, Esther and Daniel. Then we turn to the New Testament and see God Himself condescend and become a man, born of a virgin. Jesus heals the lame, gives sight to the blind and cleanses the lepers... Soon we come face to face with the fact that the God of heaven is a God of miracles... A God of action. Yet I ask you, of all of the supernatural acts recorded in Scripture, which is the greatest? It is the miracle of redemption... The application of God's own righteousness to you and I. God's greatest miracle is SALVATION.

Section One
What is a Personal Relationship with God?

What does it mean when a person claims to have a personal relationship with God? Would you claim that for yourself? Does anyone really hear from God, talk to God, or have the kind of inside track with Him that would justify such a claim? At what point does claiming to be a friend of God amount to nothing more than the ultimate form of name dropping?

It is my hope that the following pages will help to clarify this issue for you. None of us can afford to misunderstand this subject, which is as basic as it is profound.

-Dr. Clay A. Kahler

Chapter 1
You Mean You Hear God Speak?

"What do you mean there is no God? I just talked to Him this morning." This message borne by a well faded bumper sticker has nudged a few smiles along the way. But not today. One car-length back, the driver of a late-model Cadillac curses under his breath about being stuck behind a sluggish Toyota in heavy traffic. He's even more irritated having to eat the fumes of a religious fanatic. He doesn't find the sticker funny, or cute, or even honest. He has a hard time with those who talk so casually about:

- Meeting God
- Knowing God
- Hearing God
- Talking to God
- Being led by God

It's not that the driver of the big car doesn't believe in God. Like most people, he's no atheist. He knows what the inside of a church looks like. His wife is religious. And without her knowledge, he has even asked heaven for a little consideration from time to time when facing a tough business deal or even a critical shot on the golf course. Sure he prays, but he's not about to claim that he has a personal relationship with God. He's suspicious of those who do. He suspects that they are indulging in the ultimate kind of name dropping.

Yet in reflective moments he sometimes wonders if there's something he's missing. What could it mean to have a personal relationship with God?

Where Does Such an Idea Come From?

The Bible doesn't refer to a personal relationship with God. Not in those exact words. But it does show the importance of learning to know, love, and trust a very *personal* God. While you won't find the words *personal relationship* in the Bible, the idea is everywhere. Page after page suggests that it is *who* you know that counts, and that the *who* we need to know is God.

Jesus Himself prayed to His Father, "This is eternal life, that they may know You, the only true God, and Jesus Christ whom You have sent" (Jn. 17:3).[1] Commenting on this verse, theologian J. I. Packer wrote, "What were we made for? To know God. What aim should we set ourselves in life? To know God. What is the 'eternal life' that Jesus gives? Knowledge of God. . . . What is the best thing in life, bringing more joy, delight, and contentment than anything else? Knowledge of God."[2]

Many centuries earlier, the prophet Jeremiah quoted the Lord as saying, "Let not the wise man glory in his wisdom, let not the mighty man glory in his might, nor let the rich man glory in his riches; but let him who glories glory in this, that he understands and knows Me" (9:23).

What is a Personal Relationship With God?

In the following pages we will see that a relationship with God has many of the same characteristics that mark a personal

---

[1] Salvation is a personal experience; one comes to know Jesus Christ through faith. Note Christ's definition of salvation in John 17:3. It is not enough simply to know about Christ; we must know Him personally (Phil. 3:10). When we put our faith in Him, He gives us His righteousness (2 Cor. 5:21), and He becomes our Savior. It is a personal experience.
[2] Packer J. I., *Knowing God*, InterVarsity Press, Downers Grove, 1973, p.29.

relationship between two friends. These factors include some degree of:

- Mutual recognition-each knows the other.
- Mutual openness-each approaches the other.
- Mutual interests-each shares with the other.
- Mutual respect-each honors the other.

Such a relationship means more than knowing *of* or *about* someone. We might say that we know the governor of New York. But if the chief officer of that state can't pick us out of a crowd, if we can't get access to him, or if he has never shared our thoughts, feelings, and decisions, then we are claiming a friendship we don't really have.

A relationship with God is similar. If our friendship is real, we will welcome God into our lives. Our actions will show we believe He is the kind of person we want in our homes, in our plans, in our laughter, and in our tears.

With these possibilities in view, let's take a closer look at the marks of a personal relationship with God.

A Spiritual Relationship

There are those who say they have encountered God visibly, heard Him speak audibly, and felt His touch physically.

Such experiences are possible. Both Old and New Testaments are marked by miraculous, life changing encounters with God (Is. 6:1-8). He has shown, through the pages of Scripture that He is free to reveal Himself in any way He chooses.

These supernatural encounters, however, were the exception rather than the rule. While prophets like Isaiah, Moses, and Ezekiel had life changing visions of God, they did not spend the rest of their lives teaching others to have similar experiences.

In some ways it would be nice to believe that a relationship with God means experiencing the shaft of light pictured on the front of a Christian booklet. But as a rule, the truth is far less dramatic.

To meet God doesn't mean we have to see Him visibly. We do not need to wait for visions or life changing dreams. We can encounter God with the eyes of our understanding. Because He is an all powerful, ever-present Spirit, He can reveal Himself to us at a deeper level than our physical senses. The One who made the world is more than able to give insight about Himself to anyone who wants to know the truth in order to do it (Jn. 7:17; Eph. 1:17-18). He can also withhold light from those who are more interested in avoiding the truth than in finding it.

To hear God doesn't mean we have to hear Him audibly. There are times when we might wish God would break the silence and whisper in our ear. Or maybe we're glad He doesn't. In either case, it's not necessary for Him to do so. If we hear only silence, it is our own self-imposed silence.

For those who want to hear, God can be heard speaking constantly through the timeless wisdom of His Book. There and through nature (Ps. 19:1-11), He is always talking to us.

Our problem usually is not that God is not speaking, but rather that we're not sure we want to hear what He has already said.

For that reason, we need to take seriously the words of the author of Hebrews, who wrote, "Therefore, as the Holy Spirit says: 'Today, if you will hear His voice, do not harden your hearts as in the rebellion'" (3:7-8). Our opportunity to hear Him on every page of the Bible is a privilege that carries a great degree of responsibility.

To be close to God is not a matter of location. It is common to think that we must go to church to meet God. That makes sense. We meet friends at predetermined times and places. Yet, while God does use scheduled services and addresses, He is not limited to them. He promises to meet us in places of the heart. He wants us to make our hearts His home.

James recognized this when he said, "Draw near to God and He will draw near to you" (Jas. 4:8). He didn't say anything about where to go. He didn't tell us to find the highest hill in our area, or a quiet church sanctuary. Instead, James told us to humble ourselves before the Lord (4:10). He gave us reason to believe that wherever we seek Him, the Lord will meet with us there.

David, the songwriter, king, and "man after God's own heart," shows us why this is true. Deeply humbled by the Lord's constant, unavoidable presence (Ps. 139:1-6), he prayed, "Where can I go from Your Spirit? Or where can I flee from Your presence? If I ascend into heaven, You are there; if I make my bed in hell, behold, You are there. . . . If I say, 'Surely the darkness shall fall on me,' even the night shall be light about me; indeed, the darkness shall not hide from You . . . . When I awake, I am still with You" (Ps. 139:7-8,11-12,18). Nearness to God is not an issue of location. It is a matter of whether we have place in our hearts for Him. A friend of mine shared a story with me that illustrates this point so well. As she was driving with her four year old daughter to a doctor's appointment, she began to cry. Her daughter said, "What's wrong mommy?" She replied, "well honey, mommy is just a little scared right now." Without another word, the little girl folded her hands and bowed her head and prayed, "Dear God, my mommy is a little scared now… Would you please come down here?"

To know God is not a matter of knowing all about Him. That might be the greatest understatement of all. To know God is not to master Him. At best, we can exclaim with the apostle Paul:

> Oh, the depth of the riches both of the wisdom and knowledge of God! How unsearchable are His judgments and His ways past finding out! "For who has known the mind of the LORD? Or who has become His counselor?" (Rom. 11:33-34).

Given the limitations of life, our minds can barely begin to grasp the meaning of words that describe God words like *eternal*, *infinite*, *all powerful*, *all knowing*, and *everywhere present*. Yet, because He has made it possible to know Him, we can begin a process of discovery now that will never end.

We can know God because He has come to us, on *our* terms, to invite us to Himself on *His* terms. According to eyewitnesses of the New Testament Gospels, God revealed Himself to us in a person who walked on water, controlled the skies, healed withered limbs, restored sight, and stopped bleeding sores. He fed thousands with a small amount of food, drove out demons, raised the dead, loved deeply, and taught wisely.

Living a sinless life, He fulfilled Old Testament predictions, claimed to be the promised Messiah, and sacrificed His own life to secure forgiveness of sins for all who would trust Him. It was this person, known ever since as Jesus the Messiah, who said, "He who has seen Me has seen the Father" (Jn. 14:9).

So, according to the Bible, not only is a personal relationship with God a spiritual relationship, it is a Christ-centered relationship.

Chapter 2
A Christ-Centered Relationship

Mediators often play an important role in helping to resolve family, labor, and legal disputes. When emotions flare, insight is lost, communication stops, and stubbornness sets in. In such instances, an arbitrator can often bring renewed perspective and a plan for resolution.

The ultimate mediator is Christ. Nowhere is a personal go between more needed than in resolving the conflict and estrangement between man and God. Our personal sin has dug out a chasm so deep and wide that it is impossible for any of us to "cross over" to God on our own. Without a mediator, we can never overcome the alienation of affection and disruption of communication that have come between us.

God is in some ways like a parent who watches his runaway son or daughter become hopelessly entangled with the law. As much as the parent would love to wrap his arms around the child and bring him home, he can't. The law has to be satisfied. Justice must be carried out. A debt to society must be paid and a law must be enforced. For such a need, Christ has come to mediate peace between ourselves and God (1 Tim. 2:5).

Words cannot do justice to the importance of the mediating role of Christ. Without His intervention on our behalf, we could never resolve our differences with God (Jn. 14:6). Without the urging of His loving Spirit, we would never want to.

Jesus deserves our unending appreciation, admiration, and affection. When He wiped out our debt to the law by absorbing our punishment, He proved Himself to be a friend without equal. When He rose from the dead to be life and help to all who trust Him, He gave us a basis for undying hope. When He ascended to the Father's right hand to intercede for us and to act as our personal advocate, He assured that He would provide for us what no mere religion or system of belief could ever offer. He has given Himself to be the solution to our every problem, to reveal God to us, and to lead us to a personal relationship with His Father.

Christianity is Christ. As W. H. Griffith Thomas points out in a book by that title, this is the real heart of our Christian faith. We have not been called to a system of laws, traditions, and inspirational ideas. We haven't been called to the church, to a moral cause, or to the golden rule of Christian love. We have not even been called to the Bible. We have been called to Christ, the mediating person of whom the whole Bible speaks.

The apostle Paul understood the necessity of a Christ-centered relationship with God. In 1 Corinthians 1:1-9, he made it clear that he was not promoting a system of ideas. He was speaking of a relationship with God based on:

- Christ whom we serve (v.1).

- Christ who sets Christians apart (v.2).

- Christ on whose name Christians call (v.2).

- Christ who is our Lord (v.2).

- Christ who gives us grace and peace (v.3).
- Christ who brought us the grace of God (v.4).
- Christ who has enriched us in every way (v.5).
- Christ who is confirmed by experience (v.6).
- Christ for whom we eagerly wait (v.7).
- Christ who will keep us to the end (v.8).
- Christ who will have His day (v.8).
- Christ to whom God has joined us (v.9).

Paul's obsession was not a system of new thought, an ethic, a teaching, a form of church organization, denomination, or a new program. It was the person he had come to know as the one mediator between God and man (1 Tim. 2:5). It was the person who had not only died to pay for Paul's sins (1 Cor. 15:3), but also the person who, through His Spirit, was living His life through Paul (Gal. 2:20) and was his very life (Phil. 1:21).

Are we as Christ-centered as Paul? Do we realize that true Christianity is found in the living person and personality of the resurrected Christ? Have we learned that Jesus Christ is and must be at the heart of a personal relationship with God? Have we realized that no matter where we look, Christ is there?

- Look back—He is our Creator (Col. 1:16).

- Look ahead-- He is our Judge (2 Cor. 5:10).

- Look up-- He is Savior and Lord (Phil. 2:5-11).

- Look down-- He is our Sustainer (Col. 1:17).

- Look right-- He is our Teacher (Mt. 23:8).

- Look left-- He is our Advocate (1 Jn. 2:1).

- Look within-- He is our Life (Gal. 2:20).

There is no question that a personal relationship with God must be a Christ-centered relationship. It is Christ and Christ alone who can bring us to God, cleanse us from the constant pollution of the world, and be our ever present source of life and help.

It is Christ, the living Word, who reveals, defines, and expresses the personality of the Father. It is Christ who should continually be in our thoughts as Lord and Life. It is Christ who, by His Spirit, is a constant presence in and with all who have put their faith in Him (Mt. 28:19-20).

A Submissive Relationship

Any husband who is content to be just "one of the boys" in his wife's eyes isn't much of a husband. Neither is a woman much of a wife if she is satisfied to be just "one of the girls."

The intimacy of the marriage relationship carries with it a great sense of mutual commitment that will have a bearing on all of the couple's other activities and relationships.

For far greater reasons, the Designer of human personality is also not satisfied to be just "one of the gods" (Ex. 20:1-6). Yahweh, Provider and Deliverer of Israel, the God who came to us in Jesus the Messiah, will not accept a place on the shelf alongside Ra, Krishna, Moon, Allah, GM, or CBS. He has always been a jealous, possessive, commanding God. He will not share His honor with anyone else because no one else deserves that honor (Isa. 48:11).

God is to be feared more than all others. Most of us do not even like to think about things that frighten us. Whether we're talking about public speaking, high places, cramped spaces, dark nights, noises at the door, or creaks in the attic, the very thought can make us jumpy. Yet without fear, life would be very difficult. Even the animal world is endowed with an alarm and escape mechanism that provides the creature some degree of fight or flight necessary for survival.

At no time, however, is the emotion of fear more important or more neglected than when it involves our fear of God. To the extent that we know Him, we will also fear Him. Yet it is a fear, when understood, that calms all other fears and drives us to the Lord, not away from Him. It is a fear that teaches us to love, trust, and enjoy Him.

This fear might be described as the first step to a personal relationship with God. According to Solomon, "The fear of the LORD is the beginning of knowledge" (Prov. 1:7). In other words, the fear and knowledge of God go hand in hand.

Nothing and no one deserves to be feared more than the Lord. Not people, not governments, not disease, not death, not even Satan. Many who don't know God can't understand this. They assume that the Lord is the only one in the universe who *doesn't* need to be feared because He is too good and too loving to do us any harm. The ironic result is that such persons often end up missing the very love they seek because their lives are full of fear -- fear of failure, fear of people, fear of natural disasters, and fear of accident, disease, and death (Dt. 28:58-68).

Those who really know the Lord take Him seriously. They realize that God expects to be listened to when He warns about moral and spiritual failure (Prov. 8:13; 16:6). He alone determines whether anything or anyone else will be allowed to touch or test us (Job 1); and most important, He alone determines where we will spend eternity (Mt. 10:28; Rev. 2:10; 20:1-15). Such authority deserves our respect and fear.

Although we reverence God and stand in awe of His great power, at the same time we can have strong confidence (Prov. 14:26). With David we can say, "I sought the LORD, and He heard me, and delivered me from all my fears" (Ps. 34:4). A couple of verses later David added, "The angel of the LORD encamps all around those who fear Him, and delivers them. Oh, taste and see that the LORD is good; blessed is the man who trusts in Him! Oh, fear the LORD, you His saints! There is no want to those who fear Him" (Ps. 34:7-9).

That comes from someone who knew his God. It comes from someone who personally experienced that the God who asks for our surrender is a God who wants us to fear Him for our own good (Jer. 32:37-39).

God is to be loved, trusted, and obeyed more than all others. Obedience, like fear, is something we tend to resist. Yet, seeing the importance of such obedience is just a matter of perspective. For example, most of us are happy to obey a stranger's directions when we're in an unknown area. We don't even think of it as obedience. We see it more like accepting help. That's the way we can look at obedience to the Lord. It is a way of accepting His help and His love that we so desperately need. Obedience is a way of showing that we really do know the Lord and that we are growing in our knowledge of how good, loving, and wise He is.

The apostle John wrote:

> Now by this we know that we know Him, if we keep His commandments. He who says, "I know Him," and does not keep His commandments, is a liar, and the truth is not in him. But whoever keeps His word, truly the love of God is perfected in him. By this we know that we are in Him. He who says he abides in Him ought himself also to walk just as He walked (1 Jn. 2:3-6).

The fear, trust, and obedience involved in knowing the Lord do not leave us the way we were. They make us better because Christ lives within. They change us until this relationship possesses us and dominates us--bringing us heart to heart and face to face with the God of all goodness and light.

A Mutually Felt Relationship

Road worn, paw sore, and unnerved by children's stones and the nervous yipping insults of small pampered housedogs, the German Shepherd stray followed the stranger from a safe distance. Head low, and with an occasional look to the side, he stepped lightly and painfully in the tracks of the man who had thrown him half a bagel near the garbage bins of Ol' Blue's Diner. Cold, hungry, and longing for attention, the dog watched the stranger's every move, waiting for one more sign of recognition, the faintest chance for friendship. But it never came.

There are people who, when thinking about God, feel like this unwanted stray. They long for the assurance that God would smile and move toward them. But they assume Him to be too selective to feel anything for them. Some even see Him as an unchanging, eternal spirit who lives far above the ever-changing winds of pain and emotion that blow in and out of our lives.

But that is not true of the God of the Bible. The Scriptures assure us that He feels deeply for the most broken, road worn, and dejected people. He cannot be touched by our strength, but only by our weakness. While God's character never changes, His affections do change.

To know God is to affect Him. While God knew us, loved us, and chose us along with all His people in eternity past (Eph. 1:3-6), He relates to us personally and presently in a very intimate way. He rejoices with us when we are happy, sorrows when we are sad, and grieves when we are bad.

He has made Himself just that vulnerable to us. He has exposed His own heart to all of the loveless and heartless things that we do to Him. The Bible tells us that God can be:

- Pleased (Heb. 11:5).

- Grieved and sorrowful (Gen. 6:6; Eph. 4:30-32).

- Provoked and tested (Ps. 78:40-41).

- Burdened and wearied (Isa. 43:24).

- Angered, agitated, and furious (Ezek. 16:42-43).

Specifically, Ephesians 4:30-32 says, "Do not grieve the Holy Spirit of God, by whom you were sealed for the day of redemption. Let all bitterness, wrath, anger, clamor, and evil speaking be put away from you, with all malice. And be kind to one another, tenderhearted, forgiving one another, just as God in Christ forgave you."

The greatest evidence of His decision to make Himself vulnerable to us is found in the personal pains and sorrows of the One who with His own mind and heart revealed the Father to us. In the face of Jesus Christ, we find the face of God. He is the One who suffered for us so He could bring us to the Father. He loves us that much!

It might be hard for us to personalize that kind of love when we know we are only one in a world of more than 5 billion people. But we need to keep in mind who it is we are talking about. God does not have our limitations. He is not confined to human, one-at-a-time relationships. Rather, the One who made the world is able to relate intimately to as many of us at the same time as He desires.

How do we know God has that kind of capacity? We might come to that conclusion by reflecting on the size and complexity of the universe He created. Or we might consider the vast amounts of knowledge and information that finite people like ourselves can amass through the global Internet. Or we might simply trust the words of the One who said:

> Are not two sparrows sold for a copper coin? And not one of them falls to the ground apart from your Father's will. But the very hairs of your head are all numbered. Do not fear therefore; you are of more value than many sparrows (Mt. 10:29-31).

If a sparrow doesn't fall to the ground apart from His knowledge, then the One who numbers the hairs of our head is also counting the tears, the moments of our fears, and the depth of the swirling waters threatening to engulf us.

If God knows us with this kind of knowledge, then we are never as alone as we feel. We are never without help. We are never out of the Father's reach. Even though He might test our faith and our patience by not responding immediately in the way we want Him to, we can be reassured with a peace and confidence that can calm the turbulence within and lead to dramatic changes in us.

To know God is to be affected by Him. Think for a moment about the people who have changed your life for the better. Maybe it was the teacher who inspired you to go for your dreams. Maybe it was the parent or grandparent whose words and hugs made you feel deeply loved. Maybe it was the neighbor who showed you by his example that any job worth doing is worth doing well. Looking back, you can see that knowing these people changed your life.

What is true of these people will be even truer of those who come to know God. No one can know Him without being changed by Him. Anyone who comes into God's presence will be touched and changed by the One who loves us enough to accept us as we are, but loves us too much to leave us that way. The apostle James described such a personal relationship with God like this:

> Therefore submit to God. Resist the devil and he will flee from you. Draw near to God and He will draw near to you. Cleanse your hands, you sinners; and purify your hearts, you double-minded. Lament and mourn and weep! Let your laughter be turned to mourning and your joy to gloom. Humble yourselves in the sight of the Lord, and He will lift you up (4:7-10).

To know God in this way means allowing our hearts to be broken by the things that break His heart. It means finding joy in the things that bring Him joy, discovering strength in His strength, and receiving hope in the assurance that nothing is too hard for Him. It means finding a new lease on life in One who offers us forgiveness in exchange for our repentance, comfort in trade for our sorrow, and the promise of a world to come for our willingness to release our grip on this present one.

We are changed as we discover that to know God is to love Him. To love Him is to give Him first place in our hearts. Giving Him first place is to care about those He cares about, to love what He loves, to hate what He hates, and to join Him in the family business of redeeming broken lives.

This is the kind of healthy relationship that God calls us to. But such maturity doesn't just happen. Sometimes a personal relationship with God remains a faint glimmer of what it was meant to be. Sometimes we stop short of the growth to which God calls us.

A Growing Relationship

Who could doubt the personal relationship between parents and their newborn baby in the hospital nursery? Yet a one-sided parent-infant relationship provides an important counterbalance to much of what we've said up until now. On earlier pages we've emphasized the mutual nature of a relationship. Now we need to see the other side of this truth.

Just as some babies do not grow and thrive, many children of God follow a similar pattern. Sometimes growth starts and then stalls. Even though God Himself is committed to bring us to eventual maturity, He often allows us to remain infantile in our attitudes and knowledge of Him.

The apostle Paul addressed this issue of immaturity and lack of growth when he wrote:

> I, brethren, could not speak to you as to spiritual people but as to carnal, as to babes in Christ. I fed you with milk and not with solid food; for until now you were not able to receive it, and even now you are still not able; for you are still carnal. For where there are envy, strife, and divisions among you, are you not carnal and behaving like mere men? (1 Cor. 3:1-3).

Expect a process. Growing to maturity takes equal amounts of diligence and patience. On one hand, we must never be satisfied with the level of our relationship and knowledge of God. If we are, we'll stagnate, sour, and go backward. On the other hand, we must be patient with ourselves and not expect more than God expects of us.

Scripture shows that this maturity doesn't happen overnight. It requires time--time with God, and time in His Word. For that reason Peter wrote, "As newborn babes, desire the pure milk of the word, that you may grow thereby, if indeed you have tasted that the Lord is gracious" (1 Pet. 2:2-3). James supported the progressive nature of this relationship with God when he wrote, "My brethren, count it all joy when you fall into various trials, knowing that the testing of your faith produces patience. But let patience have its perfect work, that you may be perfect and complete, lacking nothing" (1:2-4).

Don't rush the process. But don't let it stop. Continue to feed on the Word of God even as you allow Him to show Himself faithful in the seasons, tests, and troubles of life. Don't expect perfection. We will fail. Be content to be learning and growing. Don't be like the homeowner who planted a garden, only to dig it up 2 weeks later because he didn't have tomatoes yet.

Expect change. Because of the very nature of spiritual life, our relationship with the Lord will change. It will change because as we go forward we will always find more--more knowledge and experience of God that will stretch us, enlarge our hearts, and make us better.

Our relationship with God can also change for the worse, however, if we begin to coast and rely on past experiences with Him. We must expect change because our relationship with Him is by nature a contested issue. Our adversary, the devil, won't be satisfied until he neutralizes us and we slip into a spiritual coma (Eph. 6:10-13).

Although our personal relationship with God can never be lost, the characteristics of that relationship will change. We will change. Count on it. Our hearts will either grow warmer or colder. Our character will either deepen or thin out. Our conversations with God will either become more intimate or less meaningful and less frequent.

Allow for incompleteness. Speaking of our incomplete relationship with God, Paul said:

> For we know in part and we prophesy in part. But when that which is perfect has come, then that which is in part will be done away. . . . For now we see in a mirror, dimly, but then face to face. Now I know in part, but then I shall know just as I also am known. And now abide faith, hope, love, these three; but the greatest of these is love (1 Cor. 13:9-10,12-13).

That's the realism we're faced with. Our knowledge and experience are incomplete. It's as if we are looking at the face of God through a clouded glass. But then it will be face to face. In the meantime, we have our orders. We must accept our incompleteness, trust God, and put our hope in His imminent return. We are to love God and His imperfect family with all of our heart. We can't afford to demand perfection of ourselves. Neither should we demand it of others. The holiness and growth that God is looking for will be seen in our brokenness and humility, not in our spiritual perfection.

Don't expect heaven now. Not only is it important for us to give ourselves time to grow in the Lord, but it is also essential that we take time to let Him show Himself absolutely faithful and satisfying to us. But don't expect in this life what He has promised to complete in eternity.

We who trust in Christ are people of eternity. There are no time limits on our future. We are not like the professional athlete who has to reach his goals and make his money and a name for himself in just a few short years before he loses his competitive edge.

Having a relationship with God is not a way to get everything we want in life. It is not the key to financial success, good health, and long life. It is, however, the way to find increasing amounts of inner love, joy, peace, patience, kindness, goodness, faithfulness, and self-control (Gal. 5:22-23). It is a means of finding the ultimate relationship, the ultimate purpose, the ultimate mission, the ultimate security, the ultimate hope.

All that remains for us is to trust Christ for what we cannot now see or have. We need to believe that what Christ said to His disciples is still true:

> Let not your heart be troubled; you believe in God, believe also in Me. In My Father's house are many mansions; if it were not so, I would have told you. I go to

> prepare a place for you. And if I go and prepare a place for you, I will come again and receive you to Myself; that where I am, there you may be also (Jn. 14:1-3).

That is our hope. We should not expect the Lord to give us everything we crave now. While He has promised to provide for the needs of all who follow Him, He also reserves the right to determine what we need now and what we will be able to enjoy more if it is deferred until later.

A Shared Relationship

We all come to God one at a time. In a sense, we come all alone. It is our personal decision, our choice, whether or not we are willing to enter into a personal relationship with God. No one else makes this decision for us. But it doesn't stop there. Once we come to God, we are joined to Him and born into His family.

Those who love God will love one another. It is impossible to have a personal relationship with God without also having Christ-centered relationships with other people. Christ's love shown on the cross is our example. He showed us that to be close to the Father means to share the Father's love for others (1 Jn. 4:7-11). As I get to know the Lord, I will also be confronted with a God who dearly loves those people around me--my family, friends, neighbors, business associates, acquaintances, and even my enemies.

This is the kind of attitude that Paul encouraged in the Christians at Thessalonica. After affirming the reality and evidence of their relationship to God (1 Th. 1:1-7), he went on to say:

> Concerning brotherly love you have no need that I should write to you, for you yourselves are taught by God to love one another; and indeed you do so toward all the brethren who are in all Macedonia. But we urge you, brethren, that you increase more and more (4:9-10).

We might like to live in isolation, but we can't do it if we're going to grow in our relationship with God. Knowing God doesn't mean just knowing about Him; it means entering into Him--into His thoughts, His heart, His sacrificial love.

The apostle John wrote:

> Beloved, let us love one another, for love is of God; and everyone who loves is born of God and knows God. He who does not love does not know God, for God is love (1 Jn. 4:7-8).

Those who love God are dependent on one another. In Ephesians 4, Paul made it clear that our vertical relationship with God is accompanied by many horizontal relationships. He pictured each child of God as a member of the body of Christ.

Each part has a function. Just as the eye, ear, mouth, and foot make distinct contributions to our physical bodies, so each believer plays a distinct role in the church, the body of Christ. When every part does its share, the whole body receives the benefit (see 1 Cor. 12 and Rom. 12).

Even though we have received a complete salvation in Christ, there is another sense in which we are not complete without relating to and serving one another. We need one another just as much as the mouth needs the eye and the eye needs the hand. This is the outworking of our salvation. We might think we are independent spirits who can do just fine on our own, but we will soon discard that idea as we grow in our knowledge of God.

Those who love God will submit to one another. In Ephesians 5:21, Paul said that we are to submit to one another in the fear of God. In the counsel that follows, his words become very specific. He tells us that:

- Wives are to serve their husbands as a means of serving the Lord (5:22).

- Husbands should lovingly surrender their own interests in behalf of their wives as Christ lovingly surrendered His interests in behalf of the church (5:25-28).

- Children are to obey their parents in the Lord (6:1).

- Servants are to be obedient to their masters as a means of serving the Lord (6:5-7).

- Masters are to show consideration for their servants out of deference to the Lord (6:9).

The message comes through clearly. Knowing God and His love (Eph. 3:14-21) means that we will lovingly and submissively serve others. As we trust God and obediently serve others, we will discover deep within our own souls the righteousness, wisdom, and power of the love of Christ.

Obediently channeling God's love to others enables us to begin to experience the meaning of Paul's prayer in Ephesians 3:14-19.

> For this reason I bow my knees to the Father of our Lord Jesus Christ, from whom the whole family in heaven and earth is named, that He would grant you, according to the riches of His glory, to be strengthened with might through His Spirit in the inner man, that Christ may dwell in your hearts through faith; that you, being rooted and grounded in love, may be able to comprehend with all the saints what is the width and length and depth and height--to know the love of Christ which passes knowledge; that you may be filled with all the fullness of God.

Chapter 3
One Who Was Close... Yet So Far Away

It is possible to be close to Christ, yet so far from the life He offers. This was true even among the original 12 apostles of Christ. They had the most obvious opportunity for a personal relationship with Him. Yet even in that inner circle, there was one, probably the most trusted member of the group (for he kept the money), who never really had the kind of personal connection with Christ that we are talking about. Judas knew a lot about Jesus. He knew the Teacher's habits well enough to lead Jesus' enemies to a garden meeting place. He knew Christ well enough to betray Him with a kiss of greeting. But Judas didn't know Jesus as his Savior and Lord.

Trusted though he was, the "keeper of the money" never had the kind of personal, Christ-centered relationship with God that is available to us today. He is a troubling example of the kind of person Jesus talked about when He said:

> Enter by the narrow gate; for wide is the gate and broad is the way that leads to destruction . . . . Many will say to Me in that day, "Lord, Lord, have we not prophesied in Your name, cast out demons in Your name, and done many wonders in Your name?" And then I will declare to them, "I never knew you; depart from Me, you who practice lawlessness!" (Mt. 7:13,22-23).

Let's make sure that we do not end up as one who presumed that to know *about* Christ is to know Him personally.

Making It Personal

Someone has said, "Knowing Christ died--that's history. Believing He died for me--that's salvation." A personal relationship with Christ begins at the moment of our salvation. Jesus referred to this event as a second birth (Jn. 3:3). Only when we are born spiritually into God's family do we become His children, His friends, His servants, and members of His spiritual kingdom.

While we may not know exactly when this new life begins, we can understand the steps we need to take to begin this relationship.

FIRST STEP: We need to admit our lost condition. All of us are born to the parents of a fallen humanity. We come into this world separated from the life of God and absorbed with an interest in finding satisfaction, significance, and personal independence on our own terms. In the process, we don't show a natural desire for the kind of God who made us for Himself (Rom. 3:11-12).

While we may look good to ourselves as long as we measure ourselves by ourselves, Jesus Christ showed us our sin. He is the One who showed us what it means to have a personal relationship with God. He is also the One who said that He didn't come into this world to help good people, but "to seek and to save that which was lost" (Lk. 19:10).

The Bible says we all come into this physical world physically alive but spiritually dead--missing out on the quality of life for which God made us. The apostle Paul wrote, "All have sinned and fall short of the glory of God" (Rom. 3:23), "There is none righteous, no, not one" (Rom. 3:10), and "The wages of sin is death" (Rom. 6:23).

SECOND STEP: We need to know what God has done for us. The word *gospel* means "good news." The gospel of Christ is that God Himself loved us enough to send His own Son into this world to rescue us from ourselves and our sin (Jn. 1:1-4; 3:16).

The good news is that Jesus lived the quality of life that God intended for us to live. Without flaw, He loved His heavenly Father with all of His heart, soul, and mind. Without fail, He showed us what it means to love our neighbor as ourselves.

Then, to solve the problem of our lost relationship with His Father, Jesus died in our place, offering Himself as a perfect sacrifice to pay the price of sin. Because He was not only man but God our Creator as well (Jn. 1:1-14), His death was of infinite value. When He rose from the dead, He proved that He had died in our place to pay the price of all sin--past, present, and future. With one sacrifice, He paid for the least (and the worst) of our sin.

THIRD STEP: We need to personally believe and receive God's gift. While we all have earned the wages of spiritual death and separation from God (Rom. 6:23), no one can earn a relationship with God. It is a *gift* of His love and mercy and not a reward for our effort. No one is saved by trying to be good. We are saved by trusting in Christ.

This is why the apostle Paul could write, "For by grace [undeserved favor] you have been saved through faith, and that not of yourselves; it is the gift of God, not of works, lest anyone should boast" (Eph. 2:8-9; see also Rom. 4:5; Ti. 3:5).

This may sound too simple. But it takes a miracle of God's grace to break our pride and self-sufficiency. It takes God's Spirit to draw us into this kind of personal relationship. If this is your desire, this is how *you* can begin.

The actual words we say to God to receive this gift may vary (Lk. 18:13; 23:42-43). What is important is that we believe God enough to be able to say, "Father, I know I have sinned against You. I believe that Jesus is Your Son, that He died for my sins, and that He rose from the dead to prove it. Now I accept Your offer of eternal life. I accept Jesus as Your gift for my salvation."

If this is the honest expression of your heart, welcome to God's family! By simple, childlike faith you have entered into a personal relationship with the One who made you and saved you for Himself.

Section 2
Does God Grade on a Curve?

Daniel Webster once said, "The most important thought I ever had was that of my individual responsibility to God." Over 150 years later, 8 out of 10 Americans say they believe they will someday give account of themselves to God.

Another survey noted that 76 percent of those who believe in an afterlife think they have a good chance of going to heaven. But on what basis do so many of us assume we will be welcomed into God's presence? Is it because we are confident that there are a lot of people worse than ourselves?

Chapter 4
Remember the Curve?

Whether or not God grades on a curve is an important question that we will take a look at in the following pages.

I can see it as if it happened yesterday. The teacher gets up from her desk with a handful of marked papers. She walks to the blackboard, picks up a piece of white chalk, and begins to show the breakdown of test results.

The class knows she grades on a curve. The top 10 percent will earn A's, the next highest 20 percent B's, and the 40 percent in the middle will earn C's. It will be bad news for those who score D's with the next lowest 20 percent, followed by the 10 percent at the bottom who fail.

This has been a tough test. Everyone is sweating. We're all hoping that we scored comparatively well with the rest of the class.

The uneasy experience of being evaluated by how we compare and measure up to those around us is a part of life that many of us never forget.

The Ups and Downs of a Curve

As students, we may have had a love-hate relationship with the curve. The upside was that this method of grading allowed room for error, especially if the test was so hard that no one scored high. The downside was that the curve automatically put us in competition with our peers.

We also soon learned that being compared with those around us is an unavoidable fact of life. Whether we interview for a job or audition for a part in the community play, we are judged by how we measure up to others.

The idea of being graded on a curve is so much a part of our life that it even spills into common notions about the afterlife.

What happens after death is a sobering thought. Many of us feel uneasy about standing before our Creator and giving an account of how we have lived our lives. Even if we have laughed among our friends at the idea of hell, we secretly hope that there is no such place. And if there is a heaven, we hope to make it through those "pearly gates"—even if by the skin of our teeth. Our confidence may be: "I'm not as bad as a lot of people. Even though I've made my mistakes, I'm pretty sure that I'm well within 'the class average.' "

Implied in this kind of reasoning is a relative goodness that is based on how we compare with one another. We take heart in knowing that there are always others far worse than ourselves.

Furthermore, many of us resist the notion that there is something about our own human nature that would keep us out of heaven. I know a lot of "good" people. And you might be one of them. They are kind to their family members. They work hard to pay their bills on time. They're not perfect, but much of the time they try to do the right thing. They are the sort of people I would want to have as neighbors. And they have earned the approval of their friends, colleagues, and community.

THE HIDDEN DARK SIDE

There is, however, another side to human nature that also deserves our attention.

Sigmund Freud, the pioneer of modern psychology and an avowed atheist, was surprised by what he discovered about the people he observed. Many of his patients exhibited virtues in their public life. But as he probed deeper, he found hidden drives of anger, lust, and envy. Freud said it was as though he had lifted a flat stone off the top of a grassy knoll near a pond and found underneath the rock a dark world of centipedes, sow bugs, worms, and other creatures fleeing from the light.

What Freud found in his counseling practice is something most of us would rather not think about. Yet he had stumbled on a great biblical truth about human nature. The gospel of John quotes Jesus as saying something similar:

> This is the condemnation, that the light has come into the world, and men loved darkness rather than light, because their deeds were evil. For everyone practicing evil hates the light and does not come to the light, lest his deeds should be exposed (John 3:19-20).

Both the observation of human behavior and the teachings of Christ point to dark shadows within the human heart.

Alexander Solzhenitsyn, the Nobel Prize winning author, describes the universal reality of this evil when he writes:

> Gradually it was disclosed to me that the line separating good and evil passes not through states, nor between classes, nor between political parties either—but right through every human heart . . . . And even in the best of all hearts, there remains . . . an un-uprooted small corner of evil (*The Gulag Archipelago,* Vol. 2, p.597).

The Excuses We Come Up With

The extent of this fault line within us is something that most of us find difficult to think about. Because we feel uneasy facing our own wrongs, we become adept at coming up with excuses and rationalizations for our mistakes and failures.

C. S. Lewis describes how easily we look past our own faults so we can focus on the failings of others:

> This year, or this month, or more likely, this very day, we have failed to [practice] ourselves the kind of behavior we expect from other people. There may be all sorts of excuses for us. That time you were so unfair to the children was when you were tired. That slightly shady business about the money—the one you have almost

> forgotten—came when you were hard up. . . . The truth is, we believe in decency so much—we feel the Rule of Law pressing on us so—that we cannot bear to face the fact that we are breaking it, and consequently, we try to shift the responsibility" (*Mere Christianity,* pp.7-8).

It's easy for us to find extenuating circumstances for things we have done wrong. And we are not alone. All around the world today, people will appeal to a moral standard of conduct that they themselves don't live up to. The reality is that all of us fall far short of our own standards, let alone the standards of a loving and holy God (Romans 3:23; 6:23).

The Grandfather God

None of us is perfect—not in our own eyes nor in the eyes of a loving God. This might lead us to think that all that matters is "the curve." A lot of people would say, "If there's one thing I know, it's that God doesn't expect me to be perfect. I may not be a saint, but I'm certainly not a devil. I care about people and try to do the right thing most of the time. If God looks for redeeming qualities in me, I'm sure He will see more good than I can."

Such thinking sets people up to think of God as a great grandfather in the sky. Grandfathers are loving, tenderhearted, and patient. Sometimes they even smile at the mischief of their grandchildren. With a knowing smile, they remind their own sons and daughters that they too were once little handfuls.

When you combine this grandfather view of God with what we know about human behavior, it becomes even easier to assume that if God grades on a curve we will be safe in a crowd of very imperfect people.

The mix of vices and virtues in those around us reassures us that if God wants sinners in heaven, He's going to have to cut most of us a lot of slack. He is going to have to be at least as tolerant and open-minded as we are. What's more, in the competitive world of the curve, the majority of the class always passes the course. Could a loving "Grandfather God" do any less?

Chapter 5
Why Doesn't God Grade on a Curve?

Despite the widespread belief that we are safe as long as we "stay with the crowd," the Bible gives us a very different way of looking at our imperfection and how it affects our relationship with a loving and holy God. And to understand this perspective, it's important to look at the early history of our first parents' relationship with God.

The Mistake Was Fatal

Our first parents, at the dawn of human history, are described in the Bible as walking in a garden paradise with their Creator. In the cool of the day, God would visit the planet to share time and conversation with His first human beings.

According to the book of Genesis, God gave only one rule to the new couple. While encouraging them to enjoy themselves in the new home He had given them, the Creator said:

> Of every tree of the garden you may freely eat; but of the tree of the knowledge of good and evil you shall not eat, for in the day that you eat of it you shall surely die (2:16-17).

Genesis goes on, however, to say that even though Adam and Eve had only one rule to keep, they soon found themselves tempted to break it.

> So when the woman saw that the tree was good for food, that it was pleasant to the eyes, and a tree desirable to make one wise, she took of its fruit and ate. She also gave to her husband with her, and he ate. Then the eyes of both of them were opened, and they knew that they were naked; and they sewed fig leaves together and made themselves coverings (3:6-8).

In their act of disobedience, our first parents did something that would forever change not only their own lives but also the lives of all their children.

"This happened just from eating a piece of fruit?" you ask. "How in the world could such a moral disaster spring from such a small infraction?"

The answer lies in what the act represented—not the act itself. Human beings were created to have a relationship with God and to remain in loving dependence on Him. By one act of distrust and rebellion they discovered the meaning of evil. By expressing self-reliance, pride, and distrust, they had placed themselves at the center of their own universe.

Over the years it would become apparent that something profound had changed—not only in the character of the human race, but also in their shared relationship to the Creator Himself.

The Death Was Spiritual

Although shaken by feelings of shame and fear, the first couple seemed to survive their disobedience. The sun rose on a new day and Adam and Eve remained very much alive. But what about the warning of Genesis 2:16-17? God had said, "Of every tree of the garden you may freely eat; but of the tree of the knowledge of good and evil you shall not eat, for in the day that you eat of it you shall surely die."

The explanation lies in the biblical meaning of *death*. The root meaning of this word in the Bible is "separation." When a person dies physically, his soul separates from his body. But when a person dies spiritually, the spirit is separated from God, the source of spiritual life. When distrust came between our first parents and God, they immediately experienced a separation from Him they had never known before. As a symptom that something had died within them, they also began to die physically.

The Result Was Evil

Our first parents broke the one rule their Creator gave them and found themselves expelled from a perfect garden home.

The spiritual death and separation that came into their lives did not stop with them. In time, the couple had two sons. The older cultivated crops, while the other raised flocks. When the older brother felt that the Creator was showing more favor to his brother than to himself, he became angry. Driven by feelings of envy and revenge, the older son killed the younger. The first child of Adam and Eve committed the first murder.

The downward spiral happened quickly. Only two chapters later, Genesis says that "the Lord saw that the wickedness of man was great in the earth and that every intent of the thoughts of his heart was only evil continually" (6:5).

This growing malignancy shows up in wave after wave of war and violence. Those who have only heard about the Bible are sometimes surprised and even shocked by how unsanitized the Scriptures are. Incest, deception, theft, rape, and murder are just the beginning of the list of sins that punctuate and color the pages of both Old and New Testaments.

The Need Was For Mercy

In the middle of this realistic record of human nature, we find a strikingly vivid picture of a loving God. Despite the terrible consequences of rebellion against Him, we find God mercifully taking the initiative to stay in relationship with those He created in His image. Time after time, a holy God goes out of His way to stay in contact with a fallen race.

God mercifully spoke, for example, to a man named Abraham—even though he was worshiping idols. God told him to leave his home in the city of Ur and promised him that He would multiply his offspring. God assured Abraham that he would become the father of a great nation and that through him all the nations of the world would be blessed (Genesis 12:1-9).

In the generations that followed, Abraham's offspring grew to be the great nation God had promised. Delivering His people out of slavery from the greatest political power of that day, the loving Creator led them to a land of promise they could call their own.

But the road to that destination was littered with spiritual rebellion. Grumbling and ungratefulness characterized the descendants of Abraham during their wilderness wanderings. In spite of this, God mercifully and supernaturally provided for their daily needs. He fed them daily with a food called manna. And when they thought they were going to die of thirst, He gave them water from a rock. At each step of the way, God gave His people not what they deserved but patient love. This experience would later cause the whole nation to sing a song that repeated over and over, "His mercy endures forever" (Psalm 136).

The Picture Was Ours

The ancient people of the Bible passed from the scene a long time ago. Yet the picture and story of their humanity remains as fresh as the daily news.

From Adam to the nation of Israel, the people of this story stand together like our own family portrait. Again and again these people broke the law and rule of God. Yet what they discovered along the way was that in breaking the law, they were themselves broken. The Old Testament prophet repeated the principle of what God had told Adam, "The soul who sins shall die" (Ezekiel 18:20). This simple statement shows the enormity of the problem that threatened our fallen race. A problem that could only be solved by the God who loves those He created in His image.

Earlier in this chapter we talked about the common belief that God will grade all of us on a curve of personal merit and comparison with others. But grading on a curve misses the point of our predicament. Just as it would be wrong for a medical school to pass the top percentage of a class even though none of the students qualified to be a doctor, so God cannot be unfaithful to His own standards of justice.

Our problem is that by nature we are so morally flawed and broken that our only hope is for God to deal with us in mercy. To pit us against one another in a great moral "competition of the curve" would not satisfy His scales of justice.

The Bible teaches that all who are born into this world inherit the legacy and spiritual condition of our first parents.

We are all born spiritually dead and alienated from a wonderfully loving and holy God.

This condition explains not only the problems of human history in general, but also the relational and personal problems of our own lives. The Scriptures tell us that in our present state all of us have a natural inclination to avoid the truth. Even though we don't always realize it, we are inclined to resist what we could know about God by suppressing the truth about Him. Rather than turning toward the spiritual light He has provided, we turn away and create God-substitutes in an effort to replace Him with something we can control. Over time, our hearts become hard as we repeatedly ignore His kindness (Romans 1:18-32). We continue along our own way as lost sheep without a shepherd (Isaiah 53:6).

If the severity of this rebellion is not addressed in this life, there can only be the certainty of judgment in the next (Hebrews 9:27). The problem is far too great for God to simply grade us on a curve. Because we are spiritually dead, none of us, on our own, can pass the test of our accountability to God.

The Solution Was God's

If the Bible can be trusted (and it can), there are serious consequences to ignoring our spiritual condition and taking comfort in the fact that there are a lot of people worse than we are. Yet, it is also in the Bible that we find God's solution for us.

For centuries, God provided the wisdom of the Old Testament to show His people how to live and how to offer sacrifices to atone for their wrongs. These writings were revered as the Word of God and passed on within a religious community from one generation to the next. At the heart of this spiritual faith was the teaching that God would one day send a Messiah, a Savior, who would deliver His people. These predictions contained mysterious descriptions of how the Servant of the Lord would die like a sacrificial lamb to bear the sins of His people (Isaiah 53).

Eventually, according to the New Testament Gospels, the Messiah did appear. In fulfillment of many predictions, He came as "the light of the world" (John 8:12).

But the light Christ brought made Him a controversial figure. One of the most offensive parts of His teaching was that even the most religious people weren't good enough to enter into the kingdom of heaven (Matthew 5:20). The candor of Jesus was taken as an insult by the religious leaders of Israel. They considered themselves teachers of righteousness and believed that their knowledge of the law put them above the crowd.

Yet despite their unique spiritual heritage, Jesus declared that those who rejected Him—though they be "sons of the kingdom"—would be rejected from God's presence in the world to come:

> The sons of the kingdom will be cast out into outer darkness. There will be weeping and gnashing of teeth (Matthew 8:12).

According to Jesus, those who refused to admit their condition before God were risking eternal spiritual banishment from the presence of the God they thought they knew. He repeatedly warned that unless they had a change of heart they would be turned away into a darkness of everlasting regret and loss.

So, how can we pass life's final exam and escape eternal separation from God?

Chapter 6
Passing By the Grace of God

What makes the words of Christ so important is that Jesus did more than tell us that our best efforts are not enough to bring us to God. He also said He had come to do for us what we could not do for ourselves.

What Christ did for us turned bad news into good news. As we have seen up to this point, without His intervention we would all be lost. According to the Bible, if Christ had not left heaven to come to our rescue, the thought of standing before Him on the curve of personal merit and comparison would be a burden at best. The assurance of our personal comparison with others would require constant rationalization to hope that we have been "good enough."

According to the Bible, our Creator has provided His own way of delivering us from our hopeless spiritual comparisons and competition. God intervened on our behalf, and offered a solution to restore to us the relationship with Him that our first parents had lost. The solution is more than "a passing grade." It also includes a new life, a changed heart, and a future that will eventually return us to a paradise that was lost.

The Cost of God's Grace

In the New Testament letter to people in Rome, the apostle Paul eloquently expressed how costly it was for God to solve our dilemma. He wrote:

> When we were utterly helpless with no way of escape, Christ came at just the right time and died for us sinners who had no use for Him. Even if we were good, we really wouldn't expect anyone to die for us, though, of course, that might be barely possible. But God showed His great love for us by sending Christ to die for us while we were still sinners (Romans 5:6-8 LB).

The Price That Only God Could Pay

We are all moved by stories of self-sacrifice. Yet there is one act of sacrificial love in human history that stands alone—Jesus Christ's death on the cross.

Have you ever thought about what He endured on our behalf? Imagine the agony as soldiers held Him down and hammered huge spikes through His hands and then His feet.

But the physical agony was not the worst part of His suffering. As He hung suspended between heaven and earth, a great darkness came over the whole earth. In that darkness, He experienced on our behalf a judgment and separation that caused Him to cry out, "My God, My God, why have You forsaken Me?" (Matthew 27:46). His anguished words give us a brief hint of the infinite price He paid to settle our legal debt.

Never before in all eternity had the Son of God been separated from His Father. Never before had He borne the weight of guilt. Yet, in that moment of human history, Christ died for our sin.

The innocent Lamb of God paid the penalty for the guilty. He wanted so much to have us with Him in eternity that He was willing to take the punishment we deserved.

> Jesus . . . for the joy that was set before Him [eternal fellowship with us] endured the cross, despising the shame (Hebrews 12:2).

But why was Christ's death the only way we could be reconciled to a holy God?

The cross allowed God to be both just and loving in dealing with our sin. No one else had given us the life and freedom we had misused. No one else, therefore, could step forward and bear the price for our wrongs. Only by the infinite sacrifice of our own Creator could the demands of eternal justice be satisfied (Isaiah 53:4,10). Because of His own sacrifice, He was then free to forgive and acquit all who trust Him for salvation (1 Peter 2:24).

The apostle Paul said it all when he wrote:

> [God] made Him who knew no sin [Jesus] to be sin for us, that we might become the righteousness of God in Him (2 Corinthians 5:21).

The Price That Only Love Could Pay

We will never understand the extent of what Christ endured on our behalf. But the principle of His sacrifice is illustrated in a story from American history. In a tribe of Native Americans, someone was stealing chickens. The chief declared that, if caught, the offender would receive 10 lashes. When the stealing continued, the chief raised it to 20 lashes. Still the chickens disappeared. In anger the chief raised the sentence to 100 lashes—a sure sentence of death.

Finally the person stealing the chickens was caught. But the chief was faced with a terrible dilemma. The thief was his own mother!

When the day of penalty came, the whole tribe gathered. Would the chief's love override his justice? The crowd gasped when he ordered his mother to be tied to the whipping post. The chief removed his shirt, revealing his powerful stature, and took the whip in hand. But instead of raising it to strike the first blow, he handed it to a strong, young brave at his side.

Slowly the chief walked over to his mother and wrapped his massive arms around her in an engulfing embrace. Then he ordered the brave to give him the 100 lashes.

That's just a small glimpse of what Jesus did for us. In love, He became our substitute and died in our place. He overcame our inability to save ourselves by paying the price for our sins. In the illustration, a mother's life was extended by the substitute of her loving son. For us, everlasting life was bought through the priceless death of the Son of God.

There is no other solution. All our best efforts to do good are ruined by the greater problem of our spiritual death and separation from God. We are like someone floundering in deep water miles from shore and without hope of surviving on our own. Our best efforts, though sincere, still fall short of God's perfect standard.

God satisfied the death penalty for sin through the sacrifice of His Son on the cross. In this way, He was completely just in judging sin, but at the same time He showed amazing and immeasurable love for us. God used grace to do for us what we could never do for ourselves.

The Gift Of God's Grace

According to the good news of the gospel, God does not want anyone to perish (2 Peter 3:9). Out of the wellspring of His love for us, God has provided the free gift of everlasting life and of relationship with Him (Ephesians 2:8-9; Titus 3:4-5).

The Reputation of "Free Gifts"

I don't know about you, but I am skeptical about any offers of a "free gift." Why? Because I'm bombarded by them. I hear them on the radio as I drive. When I flip through my mail, I'm led to believe that I've won all sorts of free sweepstakes. When I turn on the TV, I often hear offers of something free if I call within the next 30 minutes. Telemarketers interrupt my dinner to tell me I've won free tickets to some popular vacation spot. And when I use my computer to surf the Web, annoying pop-up ads appear telling me that I'm a lucky winner and that all I have to do is "click here" to get my free gift. Yet I have discovered along the way that there is almost always a catch to these free gifts. They are bait for the unsuspecting. The motive behind them is usually not one of generosity but of tease, tempt, and trap.

It's no wonder that people may be skeptical of the New Testament when it describes forgiveness of sin, everlasting life, and heaven as free gifts.

The One Gift That Is Authentic

God's gift of salvation is different. It is a genuine offer because it has already been paid for, because we could never pay for it ourselves, and because it comes from the heart and love of God.

When gifts are given in love, all that is called for is a willingness to receive them with a grateful heart. If we offer to pay back the givers to keep from being obligated to them, we insult not only the spirit of the gifts but the people who bought them for us.

According to the Bible, God offers us the gift of eternal life out of His great love for us. If we attempt to pay for it by working our way to heaven and by being better than the next guy, we insult God's grace. In fact, we may actually be rejecting the gift of God without even realizing it. The curve of personal merit doesn't work.

Outwardly we may maintain the appearance of being an upstanding individual, but inside there is no way to overcome the fact that what we need is not justice, but rather the gift of God's love, grace, and mercy (Romans 7:21-25).

God understands this weakness far better than we do. That is why the Bible says to those who have accepted Christ as their personal Savior:

> For by grace you have been saved through faith, and that not of yourselves; it is the gift of God, not of works, lest anyone should boast (Ephesians 2:8-9).

With this brief statement the apostle Paul defined the terms and basis of God's offer. We can not earn the gift of God. We can only receive it by accepting what He has already done for us.

We must also remember that according to Ephesians 2:8 we are "saved through faith." A decision and act of faith is the one requirement of grace that we must keep in mind.

The Requirement of Grace

Responding to God's gift of salvation requires a genuine willingness to receive what God is authentically willing to give.

The Heart of the Receiver

Receiving Christ as Savior and Lord requires an honest decision of trust. It is not a theoretical and mental assent to facts about Christ. Nor is it some impulsive emotional reaction that does not include the will. If our decision to receive the gift of God is genuine, it is likely to parallel what often happens in courtship and marriage. A man and a woman are initially attracted to each other. They find time to get to know each other through relaxed conversations. Over time, they discuss their interests and life goals. Then emotion and intellect unite in a conviction that they are meant for each other. In front of a minister, the man and the woman take vows of lasting commitment.

A similar process often happens as people move toward the gift of God's offer in Christ. Many are drawn to Him initially either out of their own sense of need or because of their curiosity about His wisdom and miracles. Thoughtful people may think through some of their questions and doubts, and take a closer look at the Bible's claim that Jesus not only died for our sins but rose from the dead to prove it. Eventually a decision must be made about whether to accept or reject the offer of God.

The Decision That Must Be Made.

Those who receive the free gift of forgiveness and eternal life through Christ must first abandon all excuses for their wrongs. They must be willing to admit that their own goodness will not earn them a place in heaven. They must admit to themselves and to God that they are sinners and cannot save themselves. If they are convinced that Jesus is the Son of God, all that remains is for them to believe the good news that God has provided in Him a sacrifice for their sin.

This is the wonderful news of the Bible. Jesus Christ was as sinless as we are sinful. Yet in our place He died on a Roman cross of execution to pay the penalty for our sins. He was buried and then rose from the dead 3 days later to show that His claims were true (1 Corinthians 15:1-5).

Coming to this saving relationship with Christ requires a change of heart that is often misunderstood. When the Bible calls for "repentance," it isn't asking us to make a personal resolution to clean up our lives. To repent does not mean we have to first change our ways. It means having a change of heart about God that allows Him to bring us into a new dependence on Him.

The actual process of trusting Christ occurs simply by believing. It is an act of personal faith. Yet many have found it helpful to gather their thoughts and pray something like this:

> Lord Jesus, I want to receive You as my Savior. Thank You for dying on the cross to pay the penalty for my sin. I believe You rose from the dead to offer me Your everlasting life. Please come into my life and begin to make me the kind of person You want me to be. Thank You for giving me the gift of Your forgiveness and new life.

If these words express what is in your heart, you have made the most important discovery of your life. With your trust in Christ comes His assurance of forgiveness and eternal life.

Chapter 7
Living Beyond the Curve

Once we realize that it is hopeless to work our way to heaven, we can leave behind the curve of comparisons. Now we stand not in our own merits but in the grace and love of God. We have begun an adventure of life and discovery that will never end.

Adoption Into God's Family

The apostle Paul said that receiving the gift of spiritual life involves being adopted into a family: "You received the Spirit of adoption by whom we cry out, 'Abba, Father' " (Romans 8:15).

When we become children of God, spiritual life springs up within. Where there was once a barrier between us and God, there is now a new channel and opportunity for conversation with Him.

Before developing a personal relationship with Christ, we may have even wondered if anyone was listening when we prayed. But when Christ enters our lives, He brings a new spiritual presence into our hearts. A spiritual connection can now occur that is like a young child saying "Daddy" to his loving father.

And along with this new vertical relationship with our heavenly Father comes new horizontal relationships with other believers. New believers are full-fledged members of an eternal family, and as they grow in understanding and gratitude it isn't long before they begin to act like it.

Assurance of a New Relationship

Once we are in the family of God, we begin an up-and-down journey of learning to trust our heavenly Father in every season and circumstance of life. It isn't always easy to rely on Him. Yet slowly, and sometimes haltingly, we discover that He can be trusted with everything that is important to us. Gradually, we also grow in our appreciation for what the apostle John meant when he wrote:

> These things I have written to you who believe in the name of the Son of God, that you may know that you have eternal life (1 John 5:13).

Notice that the verse does not say that we might "hope" or "guess" that we have eternal life. Instead, John made it clear that we can "know" that we have an everlasting relationship with Christ.

In John 5:24, Jesus gave His own words of assurance to those who trust Him.

> Most assuredly, I say to you, he who hears My word and believes in Him who sent Me has everlasting life, and shall not come into judgment, but has passed from death into life.

In this verse, the Lord gave us His assurance that being adopted into God's family gives us the confidence that we have begun an adventure that will never end.

This new spiritual life needs nurture and care. Just as a newborn baby needs food, love, and affection to grow and mature, so we need to let the Spirit of God develop our appetite for spiritual insight and understanding.

Before we have spiritual life, the Bible is a closed book. Its meaning is obscure at best. But with new life in Christ, the indwelling Spirit makes it possible for the Bible to come alive. Then, as the apostle Peter wrote, we will "as newborn babes, desire the pure milk of the Word, that [we] may grow thereby" (1 Peter 2:2).

Four Key Areas of Communication

Growing in Christ means pursuing a relationship with Him. Jesus is called the "Good Shepherd" because He leads and watches over those who follow Him. He said:

> My sheep hear My voice, and I know them, and they follow Me. And I give them eternal life, and they shall never perish; neither shall anyone snatch them out of My hand (John 10:27-28).

Genuine members of the flock will follow their shepherd. But how do we actually hear His voice? Our sensitivity to His voice depends on new communication in four important areas.

God Talks to Us

As we read the Word of God, He speaks to us through His own words and self-revelation (2 Timothy 3:16).

We Talk To God

As we receive understanding from Him, we respond to Him with the affections and needs of our hearts (John 15:7).

We Talk With Our New Family

As we connect with others who share our faith in Christ, we experience mutual encouragement and motivation to love as we ourselves have been loved (Hebrews 10:24-25).

We Talk With Those Who Have Not Yet Trusted Christ

As we follow Christ, we need to remember His desire for us to be His representatives to those who have not yet believed (Matthew 4:19). One of the best ways to do this is to show our honest interest and concern for others. If they first see our changed life and then know that we are genuinely interested in them, they are more likely to be curious about the difference they see in us.

Growing in these areas of communication will show our love for Christ. He in turn will enable us, by His Spirit, to do anything and say anything that He wants us to do or say (Ephesians 5:18-19). Jesus said:

> He who has My commandments and keeps them, it is he who loves Me. And he who loves Me will be loved by My Father, and I will love him and manifest Myself to him (John 14:21).

The word *manifest* means "to make an appearance, to disclose or declare." Our Lord has chosen to reveal Himself to each of us individually. No two believers have an identical relationship with the Savior, so a cookie-cutter formula won't work. But a genuine believer will have a desire to listen to God, to respond to Him, to fellowship with other believers, and to witness to those who do not yet know Christ.

Your Own Spiritual Journey

As you begin your Christian journey let God creatively guide your path. Get a readable translation of the Bible (I recommend the New King James Version) and set aside a regular time when you can reflect on God's Word and pray. Begin attending a Bible believing church where Christ is honored and where His people honestly love one another.

As time goes on, don't forget to ask God for opportunities to share with others what Christ has done for you. Let them know that God does not grade on a curve, but that He has made it possible for them to be in His loving presence forever.

That is the good news!

Section 3
The Forgiveness of God

How can we know we have not gone too far? How can we be sure we have not made ourselves unforgivable in the eyes of God?

The answer is not found in our ability to forget, or in our ability to forgive ourselves, or even in our ability to feel forgiven. The answer is found in the extent to which God has gone to bear the pain and punishment of what we deserve.

My prayer is that in the pages of this chapter we will find a freedom of conscience that will compel us to spend the rest of our lives telling others about the wonderful forgiveness of God.

Chapter 8

River of Forgiveness

Niagara Falls, on the border of the US and Canada, plunges 160 feet into a thundering, surging river. At the brink, 379,000 tons of water a minute rush over the edge. Niagara, however, is not the largest waterfall in the world. Neither is Africa's 355-foot-high Victoria Falls. While Victoria is twice as high and twice as wide as Niagara, she is dwarfed by Venezuela's Angel Falls. Dropping 3,212 feet, Angel Falls is about 20 times higher than Niagara!

Imagine being caught in the currents above Angel, or Victoria, or Niagara. Their difference in size would make little difference. There would be a point of no return, a moment of going over the edge, and then . . . a need for heaven's mercy.

The story of personal moral failure is similar. One fall may look greater than another. But in the waters of failure, there is little difference. James 2:10 says, "For whoever shall keep the whole law, and yet stumble in one point, he is guilty of all." Once we go over the edge, all that remains is a need for mercy. All we can hope for is the kind of forgiveness King David looked for after his sexual affair with Bathsheba (2 Sam. 11). In the grip of guilt that included cover-up and murder, David cried:

> Have mercy upon me, O God, according to Your lovingkindness; according to the multitude of Your tender mercies, blot out my transgressions. Wash me thoroughly from my iniquity, and cleanse me from my sin. For I acknowledge my transgressions, and my sin is always before me (Ps. 51:1-3).

Was David unforgivable? Not according to the Bible. His story stands as a timeless reminder that a repentant person can find inexhaustible waters of mercy in the forgiveness of God.

Without the assurance of forgiveness, life can end in despair. Such was the case of a young college student. On a

Canadian hunting trip, he became separated from two friends in a raging snowstorm. Though he found refuge in a lonely cabin, he died before help could arrive. When the Royal Mounted Police found his body, they discovered a note saying:

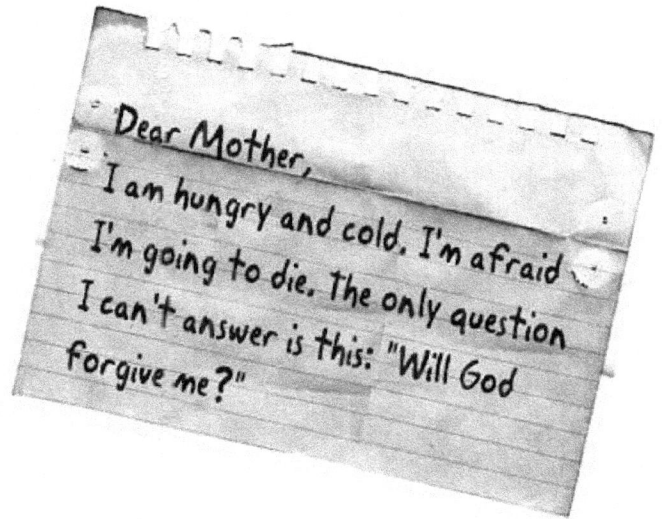

Dear Mother,
I am hungry and cold. I'm afraid I'm going to die. The only question I can't answer is this: "Will God forgive me?"

Although he was raised in a Christian home, he had become an agnostic in college. He died wondering if God would forgive him for the path he had taken.

Sometimes guilt alone makes people *want* to die. After the fatal shooting of Tejano singer Selena, the woman who pulled the trigger begged God for forgiveness. During a tape recorded conversation with police, she expressed anguish and said, "Look what I did. . . . I'll never forgive myself. . . . I don't deserve to live.'

Many of us saw another example of overwhelming guilt in the young mother who pleaded on national television for the return of her missing children. We watched when she later confessed to taking her own babies' lives.

Is there hope for those who hate themselves for what they have done? How far will God go in showing mercy? What about serial killers like Ted Bundy and Jeffrey Dahmer who claimed to find spiritual peace behind bars? While society mourned the loss of their victims, these men said before their deaths that their recent faith in Christ had given them assurance of God's forgiveness.

Can God forgive a mass murderer? Would it be moral for Him to do so? Wouldn't such forgiveness re-victimize the families and friends of those killed? Or is the more important truth that if God can forgive serial killers who throw themselves at the mercy of His Son, maybe there is hope for us all?

What about us? What if we are not so much concerned that a serial killer gets justice as we are in finding mercy for ourselves? What if we cannot forgive ourselves? What about the shame and self-contempt that is draining the life out of us? Have we crossed the line?

Chapter 9

Have We Been Too Bad To Be Forgiven?

If we believe our emotions, we may feel we have gone too far. Our self-contempt seems deserved. But there's hope. God wants us to believe in His ability to forgive sins that we cannot forget.

But what do we know about this forgiveness? What does the Bible tell us? Does it come automatically? To everyone? All the time? Not according to the Bible. God's offer of forgiveness comes with conditions. While He stands ready to forgive any brokenhearted sinner, He does not *automatically* forgive, nor is He obligated to forgive. His forgiveness does not mean that we can ignore laws of natural or legal consequence (Gal. 6:7).

The Scriptures also show there are fresh falling waters of forgiveness equal to the falls of our personal failures. In the following pages, we will see how much God has personally suffered to become "just and the justifier" (Rom. 3:26) of those who do not deserve to live. In the process we will see that:

1. God's love is equal to His anger.
2. God's mercy is equal to His justice.
3. God's forgiveness is equal to our guilt.

Through the wisdom of His love, God has found a way of satisfying the demands of His law while still offering forgiveness to the worst of sinners.

To make it easier to pass along the good news of this mercy to others, we will be working with a simple diagram to illustrate the problems and solutions of the forgiveness of God.

God's Love Equals His Anger

On July 8, 1741, Jonathan Edwards preached his famous sermon "Sinners In The Hands Of An Angry God." The congregation was so traumatized that some clung to railings for fear of sliding into the fires of hell. Edwards pleaded, "Oh sinner, consider the fearful danger you are in! It is a great furnace of wrath, a wide and bottomless pit, full of the fire of wrath that you are held over in the hand of that God whose wrath is provoked and incensed as much against you as against many of the damned in hell. You hang by a slender thread, with the flames of divine wrath flashing about it and ready every moment to singe it."

Edwards went on to say, "The misery you are exposed to is that which God will inflict, to the end that He might show what the wrath of Jehovah is. God has had it on His heart to show to angels and men, both how excellent His love is, and also how terrible His wrath is."

Edwards' emphasis on the wrath of God is foreign to our generation. Yet an amazing thing happened as he quoted heavily from Bible texts warning of the anger of God. Terrified men and women woke from their sin long enough to see their desperate need for the forgiveness of God.

God's anger is not a denial of His love. His anger means He cares too much to ignore the harm we are doing to ourselves and to one another. Woven into the greatest love story the world has ever known is the unfolding drama of a God who loves enough to hate evil. He cares enough to be angry with religionists who trivialize sin in themselves, while separating themselves from those who need mercy. He cares enough to be angry with those of us who reduce sin to petty legalisms, while ignoring the needs of others.

Because God revealed Himself in the mirror image of His Son (Col. 1:15), in Jesus we find an accurate picture of the balance between heaven's love and anger. Jesus cared enough to be angry (Mt. 21:12). He loved enough to warn us of pending judgment (Jn. 3:36), while assuring us that His love is equal to His anger (Jn. 3:16).

We cannot afford to misunderstand the relationship between the love and anger of God. Jesus did not come to condemn us (Jn. 3:17). He came to save us from our sin and from His own wrath. Long before the sermon of Jonathan Edwards, Jesus said, "Do not fear those who kill the body but cannot kill the soul. But rather fear Him who is able to destroy both soul and body in hell" (Mt. 10:28). The truth about God's love and anger is not found in one or the other. The truth is that His love is equal to His anger, and because of His love He found a way to show mercy.

God's Mercy Equals His Justice

Society is troubled when crime goes unpunished. For the murder of a child, we want the guilty to pay. For a terrorist bombing, Middle Eastern custom demands that someone settle the score. The demand for justice is deeply rooted. The God of the Old Testament established the principle of eye-for-eye, life-for-life justice in a setting of legal witnesses and due process (Dt. 19:21).

How then can this same God pardon a sinner? How can justice be satisfied except by punishment of the guilty party? Who else can be held responsible for our sin? There is only one other possibility. Other than ourselves, the only one who can be held responsible is the One who gave us the freedom to sin. Like a parent who gives use of the family car to a 16-year-old child, God gave us the freedom, the time, and the capacity to sin. Is it possible for Him to offer to pay for our damages?

According to Scripture, that's exactly what God did. At great cost to Himself, He paid the price for our sin. In retrospect, we can see how much God was planning to pay when He said, "The life of the flesh is in the blood, and I have given it to you upon the altar to make atonement for your souls" (Lev. 17:11).

Was this a veiled admission of divine guilt? Was God allowing for the possibility He had been wrong to give us moral capacity and freedom of choice? Is this why He put in motion a ritual system of sacrifice that would end up costing Him inexpressible pain? No. The last book of the Bible shows that for all eternity, the choirs of heaven will declare God holy in all He is and does (Rev. 4:8). Throughout all eternity, heaven will show that God was right in giving us freedom to sin. Eternity will show His wisdom in letting us discover the wages of sin and the terrible consequences of our willful disobedience.

Throughout all eternity, heaven will also honor the justice and mercy of the Creator who lovingly chose to bear the burden of our rebellion.

The payment for our sin came at heaven's expense. In an act of unparalleled self-sacrifice, God built a two-lane bridge of mercy and justice over the chasm of sin separating us from Him. On earth, Roman executioners drove nails into the hands and feet of God's only Son. In heaven, a Father suffered as no human father has ever suffered. When it was finished, God accepted the sacrifice as sufficient payment for our sin.

Justice was satisfied. In the eternal moments and infinite agony of the Son who cried, "My God, My God, why have You forsaken Me?" (Mt. 27:46), the Creator Himself became sin for us (2 Cor. 5:21).

Three days later, Christ rose bodily from the dead. By the miracle of resurrection He showed heaven's acceptance of His sacrifice. An endless river of mercies began flowing from the cross on which He died. A legal foundation had been laid for the doctrine of justification by faith. According to the apostle Paul, God is *just* (righteous) to *justify* (declare righteous) all who come to Christ in faith. In the third chapter of Romans, he wrote:

> By the deeds of the law no flesh will be justified in His sight, for by the law is the knowledge of sin. But now the righteousness of God apart from the law is revealed, being witnessed by the Law and the Prophets, even the righteousness of God, through faith in Jesus Christ, to all and on all who believe. For there is no difference; for all have sinned and fall short of the glory of God, being justified freely by His grace through the redemption that is in Christ Jesus, whom God set forth as a propitiation by His blood, through faith, to demonstrate His righteousness, because in His forbearance God had passed over the sins that were previously committed, to demonstrate at the present time His righteousness, that He might be just and the justifier of the one who has faith in Jesus (vv.20-26).

God's Forgiveness Equals Our Guilt

At this point, to complete the diagram, we can write *sin forgiven* and *guilt removed* in the remaining boxes. Because of the unlimited scope of Christ's death on the cross, we have received forgiveness not only for past sins, but for all sins, past, present, and future.

Once For All

The moment we trust Christ as Savior, we are given immunity from punishment. The issue is settled: Our case is closed and God will not open the files of our guilt again. As the courts of earth honor the principle of double jeopardy, so heaven will not judge twice those whose sins have been punished in Christ. We will not be tried again for the sins He bore in our place.

The wonderful truth of justification is that God by His own authority acquits us. While He does not "make" us righteous, He "declares" righteous those who have appealed to the death of Christ as payment for their sin. Because God "made Him who knew no sin [Christ] to be sin for us" (2 Cor. 5:21), God can be "just" and the "justifier" of those who accept His own payment for their sin (Rom. 3:26).

Does this mean we are no longer accountable for our wrongs? No. We are still subject to natural and legal consequences. We can still risk our reputation, health, and relationships by careless, unprincipled living. But we will not lose heaven.

We can still lose rewards and a "well done" at the judgment seat of Christ, where our Lord will hold us accountable as His children. But those of us who are in Christ will never be condemned for our sin. That is why the apostle Paul could write:

> Having been justified by faith, we have peace with God through our Lord Jesus Christ, through whom also we have access by faith into this grace in which we stand, and rejoice in hope of the glory of God (Rom. 5:1-2).

Again, it is important to remember that the word *justified* in this verse is a legal term. It was used in ancient law courts to describe the status of a person who had paid the full penalty for his crime and was restored to his place in society.

In essence, God says to the person who trusts Christ, "Your sins have been paid for. My Son died for you. Therefore, in Him you stand righteous before Me. You are forgiven of all your sin in a once-for-all transaction!"

Chapter 10

Complete

The forgiveness God offers is comprehensive. It is complete and final—not just until the next inevitable sin. This is why in another letter Paul could quote Psalm 32:1-2 when he wrote:

> Blessed are those whose lawless deeds **forgiven**, and whose sins are **covered**; blessed is the man to whom the LORD shall **not impute** sin (Rom. 4:7-8).

Let's look at three important terms in this verse which show the completeness of God's mercy.

Forgiven. Think about a young, struggling mountain climber trudging up a steep trail with a large backpack. The burden is heavy for him. He weakens and lags behind. He sinks to the ground. Then an older climber drops back, lifts the load off his back, and shoulders it himself. The young hiker feels revitalized and free and starts up the trail with joy ringing in his heart. The word translated "forgiven" means "to lift off, to carry away." That is what happens to our guilt when God forgives us.

Covered. When we trust in Christ, our sins are removed forever. The Greek word translated "covered" in Romans 4:7 means "to cover over completely, to obliterate." This means they are blotted out forever. Therefore, we do not need to worry about being confronted by those sins again. We will not see them in a rerun at the judgment. They are completely removed. This promise made to Israel applies to all who trust Christ: I, even I, am He who blots out your transgressions for My own sake; and I will not remember your sins (Isa. 43:25).

Not imputed. The word *impute* means "to charge to an account." God charges to Christ our sins, and charges to our account the righteousness of Christ. He will not hold our sins against us. They will not affect our standing in heaven. The accountability of the judgment seat of Christ will be about rewards of service gained or lost. Punishment will not be the issue.

If you have never known the forgiveness of God, it can be yours right now. All that remains is for you to personally choose to trust in the One who has done so much for you. Look up these New Testament references to be assured of what God has promised:

- John 3:16; 5:24; 6:47; 7:38; 11:25; 20:31
- Acts 13:48; 16:31
- Romans 1:16; 4:3; 5:1; 10:11

Different Kinds of Forgiveness

Once we are in the family of God, there is more to learn about the forgiveness of the Father. We learn, for instance, that more than one kind of forgiveness is mentioned in Scripture. While *forgiveness* consistently means "to loose" or "to remove" a barrier to relationship, different kinds of barriers and relationships may be in view.

1. God's Legal Forgiveness

This is God's once-for-all removal of all legal barriers to heaven. With the granting of this forgiveness, God acts as Judge to declare *all* sins "paid for in full." From this moment on, Christ is our Advocate (1 Jn. 2:1). Along with His Father, He gives us legal immunity from any accusation that could separate us from the love of God (Rom. 8:28-39).

We need to remember, however, that this forgiveness is not universally applied. It is given only to those who personalize God's mercy. Like medicine, forgiveness is not effective until taken.

2. God's Family Forgiveness

This forgiveness occurs after we have been legally pardoned and born into the family of heaven. By this mercy, God removes relational barriers to our closeness with Him. In this forgiveness, He acts not as a Judge but as our heavenly Father.

When we disobey Him and do not correct ourselves (1 Cor. 11:31), He gets our attention with painful circumstances (see Heb. 12:4-11). The discomfort is for our good. It comes from a Father who loves to "forget" our sins when we honestly confess them and agree to place ourselves back under the control of His Spirit.

This kind of forgiveness is similar to what we experience in our own families. If a son takes the family car without permission and then lies about it, his parents are not doing him a favor by acting as if it did not happen. Before driving privileges can be restored, the son must own up to his wrong and be forgiven. His status within the family is never in jeopardy (legal forgiveness), but the basis for trust has been damaged, and family forgiveness is needed.

This is the forgiveness in view in John's statement to fellow members of the family of God:

> If we confess our sins, He is faithful and just to forgive us our sins and to cleanse us from all unrighteousness (1 Jn. 1:9).

3. People-To-People Forgiveness

Our forgiveness of one another is to be patterned after the way God forgives us. From His example, we learn that while our love for others needs to be *unconditional,* there is a place for *conditional* forgiveness.

Whether or not we consider an offense a "dead issue" will be determined by whether the offending party is willing to own up to the wrong. Christ-like love makes it necessary sometimes to withhold forgiveness until the one who has done the harm admits responsibility for it (Lk. 17:1-10).

What About the Unpardonable Sin?

The Bible speaks of one unpardonable sin. Jesus talked about a blasphemy against the Holy Spirit that can never be forgiven (Mt. 12:31-32; Mk. 3:28-29). In addition, the apostle John mentions a "sin leading to death" (1 Jn. 5:16-17). What are these sins? Could we have committed them? How do we know whether we have crossed over the line?

The Blasphemy against the Holy Spirit

Jesus said, "Therefore I say to you, every sin and blasphemy will be forgiven men, but the blasphemy against the Spirit will not be forgiven men. . . . whoever speaks against the Holy Spirit, it will not be forgiven him, either in this age or in the age to come" (Mt. 12:31-32).

Before identifying the principle, let's note a couple of facts. On the positive side, only blasphemy against the Spirit is called unpardonable. Every other sin can be forgiven. That is good news.

It is also important to see the context in which Jesus made His statement. He gave His warning to religious leaders who were publicly rejecting Him. The Pharisees heard Him speak, saw His miracles, and observed His blameless life. Yet they still attributed His supernatural acts to the power of Satan. That is how they blasphemed the Spirit.

Technically, this sin cannot be repeated today in the same way it was committed in Jesus' day. Jesus is not physically with us doing miracles that can be attributed to Satan.

But can this sin be committed in principle? What if we have made irreverent remarks about the Holy Spirit? Is it possible we have committed this sin and passed a point of no return? Not if we are concerned about our relationship with Christ. A person who has committed the blasphemy Jesus was talking about will not want to be reconciled to Him. Someone in an unforgivable state would not long for the acceptance and forgiveness of the Son of God. Such a person would be like the Jewish leaders who because of their envy and stubborn pride continued to reject Jesus till their death.

Unforgivable people are those whom God has hardened in their own choices. The Holy Spirit no longer urges them to believe. These people will never long to believe in Jesus as their personal Savior. They will never worry about whether they can be forgiven.

If we are worried about whether or not God has accepted our belief in Christ, we are not unforgivable. Our concern shows that our heart is still soft and that we have not passed a point of no return.

Some might ask, "What about Esau? He tearfully showed repentance without receiving mercy" (Heb. 12:16-17). Look at the context. Esau was not begging for the everlasting forgiveness of his sins. He was crying because he had traded his family inheritance for a bowl of soup. When he realized what he had done, he found that it was too late to get his birthright back.

The Sin That Leads To Death

This is different from the unpardonable sin. A sin that results in death can be committed by the Lord's own people. The apostle Paul told believers in Corinth that because of their disrespect for "the Lord's Supper" (Communion Table), some of them were weak, some were sick, and some had even died (1 Cor. 11:30).

The apostle John also mentioned the possibility of a sin that would result in death. Without identifying any specific fatal behavior, he acknowledged in 1 John 5:16-17 the kind of sin that was committed by Ananias and Sapphira in Acts 5:1-11.

According to 1 Corinthians 11:30 and 1 John 5:16-17: (1) The sinning people who experienced premature death belonged to God. (2) Their "death" was physical, not eternal. First Corinthians 11:31-32 goes on to say, "For if we would judge ourselves, we would not be judged. But when we are judged, we are chastened by the Lord, that we may not be condemned with the world."

Chapter 11

Three Misbeliefs About Forgiveness

The teaching that the forgiveness of God comes through faith alone in Christ finds some disagreement among church people. Some say forgiveness cannot be found without emotional repentance. Others say baptism is a necessary condition. Still others say good works are a requirement. Let's see what the Bible says about such conditions.

Repentance. Some suggest that we have not met the requirements for forgiveness until we have gone through a period of tears, earnest prayer, and deep sorrow for our sin.

The New Testament does call for repentance (Mt. 3:2; Acts 2:38; 20:21), but it is not a repentance that can be measured in tears or emotions. Rather, it is something that has already occurred by the time we put our faith in Christ.

The basic meaning of the Greek word translated "repentance" is "a change of mind." We repent when we change our beliefs about God and ourselves. Rather than continuing to see ourselves as acceptable to God on our own merits, we begin to see how much we need the forgiveness of God.

If we have an overwhelming sense of God's holiness, we may feel deep sorrow for the wrongs we have done against God and others. When we think about the way Christ suffered, we may be brought to tears. But the essence of repentance is a change of mind and beliefs about our sin, and about our need of Christ-not the feelings associated with it.

If we acknowledge that our sin is against God and turn in faith to Jesus Christ, we have done all that is necessary for forgiveness. This may or may not be accompanied by a deep emotional outburst. The change of mind is essential; bitter tears and deep sorrow are not.

Baptism. Some people say we cannot be forgiven by God unless we are baptized in the right way by the right people. But the Bible makes it clear that baptism is an evidence of salvation, not a requirement for it.

People who insist on baptism as a part of salvation usually quote Acts 2:38, "Repent, and let every one of you be baptized in the name of Jesus Christ for the remission of sins." They say that if we are not "baptized . . . for the remission of sins" we cannot be forgiven.

Notice the key word *repent.* The basic condition is for us to agree with God that our sin is a violation of His moral law and to turn in faith to Jesus Christ. In addition, the preposition *for* [*eis*] in the phrase "for the remission of sins" does not mean "in order to [be forgiven]." Its basic meaning is "with a view toward" or "in relation to." When Jesus said the people of Nineveh "repented at [*eis*] the preaching of Jonah" (Lk. 11:32), He was saying they repented "with a view toward" or "in connection with" Jonah's message.

In Acts 2, therefore, Peter was telling the men of Jerusalem to repent and let themselves be baptized "with a view toward" the remission of sins. Their baptism was to be an evidence of their repentance and forgiveness, not a condition for it.

In addition, the following factors show that water baptism is not essential to salvation:

- Abraham was forgiven before he was circumcised, apart from any rite or ceremony (Rom. 4:9-10).

- Jesus declared people forgiven before they were baptized (Mt. 9:1-7; Lk. 7:36-50; 18:9-14; 19:1-9; Jn. 8:1-12).

- Cornelius and his family received the Holy Spirit before baptism (Acts 10:44-48).

- The Bible shows that forgiveness and salvation are received by faith (Jn. 3:16; Rom. 5:1; 10:1-13; Eph. 2:10).

In the light of these factors, baptism should be seen as an outward act by which we publicly identify with Christ and His church. It is not a requirement for salvation.

Good Works. "But what about works?" some people ask. "Wouldn't it be unfair for God to forgive on the basis of faith alone? Didn't James say that faith without works is dead?"

Without a doubt, good works are important to every Christian. The Bible calls for good works. But good deeds are not a condition for receiving forgiveness (see Rom. 3:27-28).

Ephesians 2:8-10 shows that rather than being a condition for forgiveness, good works are the fruit and evidence of a forgiven life. Those who are saved through faith become God's "workmanship, created in Christ Jesus for good works" (v.10).

But what about James' statement that "faith without works is dead"? James was saying that genuine faith produces good works. Christ-like actions allow us to be justified, or declared right, in the eyes of those around us. It is the way we prove the reality of our faith (Jas. 2:14-26). Our good deeds are not a part of the basis of our forgiveness but a natural result of it.

To summarize: The wonderful message of the Bible is that forgiveness comes through faith alone. It is not faith plus repentance, faith plus baptism, faith plus good works, or faith plus anything!

Some Common Questions

We should not be surprised if we continue to have questions about the forgiveness of God. We cannot easily step away from the relational and emotional issues that stubbornly refuse to be put to rest.

QUESTION 1: "What if I don't feel forgiven by God?"

Most of us struggle with feelings of guilt and shame. Long after we have confessed our sins to God, we are apt to feel unforgiven. We might fear that we have been rejected by God.

When feelings of guilt hound us-and they will-we need to remind ourselves that our forgiveness does not depend on how we feel.

Forgiven people can feel like they are hanging by a thread over the fires of hell. Forgiven people can be oppressed by the accuser of our souls (Satan), who stirs up old emotions the way we stir up the embers of a dying fire. Suddenly we are inflamed in the emotions of anxiety and despair. But those emotions are not telling us the truth about the forgiveness of God.

Forgiveness is something God does. It is not rooted in our own emotions. It does not depend on whether we forgive ourselves. Forgiveness is what God does in the books of heaven when He marks "canceled" over our debt of sin. We are forgiven when He declares us legally acquitted, regardless of how we might be feeling at the moment.

Because it is so important to realize that the forgiveness of God is something *He* does. Let's look at eight pictures of God's forgiveness as seen in the Old Testament. Author David B. Kennedy notes:

1. God bags up our sins to throw them away. "My offenses will be sealed up in a bag" (Job 14:17 NIV).

2. God blows away the sin barrier. "I have swept away your offenses like a cloud, your sins like the morning mist" (Isa. 44:22 NIV).

3. God takes away our sins. "As far as the east is from the west, so far has He removed our transgressions from us" (Ps. 103:12 NIV).

4. God treats our sin like a vanquished foe. "You will tread our sins underfoot" (Mic. 7:19 NIV).

5. God puts our sins out of His sight. "You have put all my sins behind Your back" (Isa. 38:17 NIV).

6. God puts our sins out of His mind. "I will . . . remember their sins no more" (Jer. 31:34 NIV).

7. God cancels the debt of our sin. "I, even I, am He who blots out your transgressions" (Isa. 43:25 NIV).

8. God removes sin's stain and restores purity. "Though your sins are like scarlet, they shall be as white as snow" (Isa. 1:18 NIV).

QUESTION 2: "Isn't forgiveness something between us and God alone?"

Yes. Biblically, forgiveness is very personal. No one else can decide for us whether we are going to believe in Christ for the forgiveness of our sins.

But personal does not mean private. Those who have lost the weight of sin have every reason to go public. While someone who finds gold on his land might have reason to be quiet about his discovery, someone who finds a cure for AIDS, cancer, or the common cold would be a moral criminal for holding the information to himself.

According to the New Testament, those of us who have found something more valuable than gold owe our discovery to those still struggling (Rom. 1:14-16). The eternal burden and guilt of sin is far more dangerous than AIDS.

QUESTION 3: "Why does the Bible say God will not forgive us if we don't forgive one another?"

Jesus said:

> If you forgive men their trespasses, your heavenly Father will also forgive you. But if you do not forgive men their trespasses, neither will your Father forgive your trespasses (Mt. 6:14-15).

The answer is in the context. By this statement, Jesus was not teaching lost people how to be saved. He was teaching His own disciples how to stay in good family relationship with the Father.

QUESTION 4: "Does this mean we should always forgive others unconditionally?"

No. Like so many other principles of Scripture, there is a time to forgive and a time not to forgive. While we are always to love others unconditionally (by seeking their good rather than their harm), Jesus Himself teaches us to forgive people *when* they acknowledge their wrongs (Lk. 17:1-10; Mt. 18:15-17).

We do not love well when we allow our brothers or sisters to knowingly harm us without holding them accountable.

QUESTION 5: "But what about Jesus' teaching that if we don't forgive others, He will not forgive us?"

By comparing this Scripture with other passages, we must conclude that Jesus was referring to an unwillingness to love those who have harmed us, and an unwillingness to forgive those who have repented of the wrong they have done (Lk. 17:3-4). What He will hold against us (in a family sense) is our determination to withhold from others the kindness and forgiveness that He has shown to us. This is a "family issue," not a factor that could determine our eternal destiny.

QUESTION 6: "But doesn't God forgive us unconditionally? Aren't we to forgive others as He has forgiven us?"

When the apostle told us to "be kind to one another, tenderhearted, forgiving one another, just as God in Christ forgave you" (Eph. 4:32), he made it clear that we are to pattern our forgiveness after God's forgiveness of us.

God does not forgive unconditionally. First He grants legal pardon to those who meet the condition of acknowledging their sin and believing in His Son. Then He extends family forgiveness to those sons and daughters who confess their sin and seek to be restored to the Father (1 Jn. 1:9).

QUESTION 7: "If we have been forgiven by God, why won't people let us forget the past?"

Being forgiven by God does not release us from the natural consequences of our sins. Crimes against the state must be subjected to legal due process. Acts against individuals deserve restitution. The forgiveness of God does not qualify former embezzlers to be entrusted with other people's money, just as it does not give us reason to entrust our children to someone with a history of molesting. This is wisdom.

The Effects of Guilt

When we sin and refuse to come to Christ for forgiveness, our guilt may express itself in a number of different ways. For instance, before David repented of the terrible sins of adultery and murder, he experienced physical, emotional, and spiritual anguish. In Psalm 32:3-4, describing how his guilt affected him, he wrote these words:

> When I kept silent, my bones grew old through my groaning all the day long [emotional]. For day and night Your hand was heavy upon me [spiritual]; my vitality was turned into the drought of summer [physical].

Here are some ways we may be affected by guilt.

1. Physical. Unresolved guilt may affect us physically. It usually manifests itself in one of these ways:

- listlessness
- imagined sickness
- real illness
- headaches, stomach disorders, vague pains
- exhaustion

If we try to run from our guilt, immersing ourselves in work or turning to sin in reckless abandon, we will pay a price. Eventually our bodies will force us to slow down.

2. Emotional. Psychologists and counselors see these emotional effects of guilt:

- depression

- anger
- self-pity
- feelings of inadequacy
- denial of responsibility

3. Spiritual. Unresolved guilt may have the following spiritual effects on us:

- a sense of alienation from God
- inability to pray
- reduced fellowship with believers
- no feeling of joy
- inability to read the Bible

4. Relational. A lack of forgiveness will have an impact on our relationships with others in these ways:

- irritability
- blaming others
- withdrawal
- profuse apologies
- inability to relax
- self-justification
- refusal to accept compliments
- outbursts of temper

David's entire life was affected by his guilt. It touched him physically, emotionally, spiritually, and relationally. But he cried out to God, found the assurance of forgiveness, and was able to enjoy life again-damaged but hopeful.

Would David have been more honorable not to seek God's forgiveness? Would he have been more respectful of his victim's survivors to refuse any mercy? Would self-condemnation and suicide have been a more noble course of action?

Only if there is no life beyond the grave. Only if the rest of us were not sinners. Only if a forgiven person has nothing to offer. Only if God does not love us enough to long for our restoration. But as the Scriptures show, God loves sinners.

Chapter 12

Biblical Examples of Forgiveness

Aaron. Although he was involved in making a golden calf, Aaron later was appointed head of the priesthood (Ex. 32; Lev. 8).

Aaron and Miriam. When they opposed Moses' God-given authority, Miriam was stricken with leprosy. But they confessed and were forgiven and cleansed (Num. 12).

Eliphaz, Bildad, Zophar. Although these men falsely accused Job and misrepresented God, they found forgiveness (Job 42).

Rahab. This Jericho prostitute turned to the Lord of Israel and became part of Jesus' family tree (Josh. 2; Mt. 1:5).

David. Although he was guilty of adultery and murder, David repented and confessed his sin. He was spoken of as a man after God's own heart (2 Sam. 11-12; Ps. 51).

A paralytic. To demonstrate His authority, Christ forgave and healed this disabled man (Mt. 9:28).

Matthew. This tax collector with a bad reputation became Christ's disciple (Mt. 9:9-13).

A repentant criminal. When he cried out to Jesus on the cross, this thief was welcomed into Paradise (Lk. 23:40-43).

Peter. Although he denied Christ three times, Peter became a pillar in the church (Mk. 14:66-72; Jn. 21:15-19).

A woman caught in adultery. Her accusers backed away and Christ forgave her sins (Jn. 8:1-11).

Zaccheus. This greedy tax collector climbed a tree to see Jesus and came down to receive forgiveness (Lk. 19:1-10).

Nicodemus. Officially part of the group of ruling Pharisees who provoked Christ's strongest condemnations, Nicodemus recognized Jesus as Savior and Messiah (Jn. 3:1-21; 19:39).

Paul. Killer of Christians and self-confessed "chief of sinners," Paul is a prime example of the grace of God (Acts 9; 1 Tim. 1:15).

Corinthian believers. Once they were idolaters, adulterers, homosexuals, thieves, greedy, slanderers, and swindlers, but now they had experienced God's forgiveness (1 Cor. 6:9-11).

The public sinner who washed Jesus' feet with her tears. When a religious Pharisee objected that Jesus would let such a woman even touch Him, Jesus said:

> "There was a certain creditor who had two debtors. One owed five hundred denarii, and the other fifty. And when they had nothing with which to repay, he freely forgave them both. Tell Me, therefore, which of them will love him more?" Simon answered and said, "I suppose the one whom he forgave more." And He said to him, "You have rightly judged." . . . Then He [Jesus] said to her [the public sinner], "Your sins are forgiven" (Lk. 7:41-48).

Will God Forgive Me?

The following anonymous story is a personal testimony from a believer who struggled with not feeling forgiven by God.

I had been a Christian for several years, but during that time I had occasional distressing bouts with anxiety. I just could not believe that God had actually forgiven me. Sometimes I even doubted that He was capable of forgiving a woman whose sins were as bad as mine.

I remember vividly an evening when I was looking through my photo album. As I walked back over the years, the pictures seemed to condemn me anew. They brought back to my mind the kind of life I had lived before I had confessed my faith in Christ. As I turned the pages, photo after photo leaped into focus and pointed a finger of accusation directly at me.

It all came back in huge, overwhelming waves of condemnation. The drinking (I used to brag about being able to drink anyone under the table); the smoking; the friends who swapped wives among themselves; the angry chip on my shoulder about not knowing the man who caused my birth. Then came a messy divorce, followed by a physical involvement with a man I knew I did not love.

I closed my eyes to escape the pictures. But all I could see were nails being driven into the hands of Christ. I agonized. The photo album brought all my sins back. All my Christian joy was gone. I could see only my unworthiness, the blackness of my sin, and my terrible guilt. Shame engulfed me. I felt totally worthless and condemned.

I pleaded with the Father to help me. The Bible had become a staff of life to me, so I turned to it in desperation. Was I truly forgiven of all my sins? God led me to these verses:

> Do not remember the former things, nor consider the things of old. Behold, I will do a new thing, now it shall spring forth; shall you not know it? I will even make a road in the wilderness and rivers in the desert. I, even I, am He who blots out your transgressions for My own sake; and I will not remember your sins (Isa. 43:18-19,25).

My heart welled up with joy. My smile returned, for I knew I was forgiven and that I didn't have to remember who I used to be. I realized that I am the Lord's and I am here for His glory and praise.

I know now that Satan, the accuser of the brethren, used those memories to oppress me. He wanted to cripple me, to make me ineffective in the service of God. But the truth of the Bible had once again triumphed.

When I look at my picture album now, I see the "new me"--not the one captured by past sins. I am covered forever with the robe of the righteousness of Christ!

Section 4
Our Justification by Faith

ACCEPTED BY GOD

Our Justification Through Christ

What does the Bible have to say to a person who feels too bad to be accepted by God? Or to someone who feels no need of the forgiveness that Christ offers? Or to a person who wonders how anyone on earth can make it to heaven? These are crucial questions because the Bible tells us that not only is God characterized by genuine and generous love, but He is also known for His fair and far-reaching justice. Both the Bible and our conscience remind us that we are guilty of violating God's laws. So how do we satisfy His justice? It is my hope that as you read this chapter you will discover the many reasons you have for rejoicing in all that Jesus Christ has done for you. For it is only in Him that we find the solution to how we can be accepted by God.

Chapter 13
Who Needs To Know?

Do you think we'll be surprised to see who makes it to heaven? Will we be just as surprised to see who isn't there? Can you imagine the possibility that a controversial political figure made it and your pastor didn't? What if a person you never dreamed of seeing in heaven was sitting at Jesus' feet?

Is such an outcome possible? If so, how can it be, and who needs to know what it takes to get to heaven?

Our neighbors need to know

A friend of mine told the following story: When my wife and I moved into a four unit apartment building soon after our marriage, we got to know Earle, who lived in a downstairs unit. He was a widower, retired, and opinionated. When he sneezed, the building shook to its very foundation.

Earle told me that he could believe most of the Bible, but he thought it arrogant to claim that you could be sure you would be accepted into heaven. As months went by, I continued to talk with him. Then one day Earle walked up to me, smiled, and said something like this: "You know, if you can't believe the Bible, you can't believe anything. I'm sure I'm going to heaven." Several years later as he was dying of cancer, he told me he was glad he was able to face death without fear.

In that same building where I met Earle, a young couple with two small children moved into the apartment below us. They accused me of idolatry because I used the English names God and Jesus instead of the Hebrew names. They spoke of Jesus as being the true Messiah, the only acceptable sacrifice for our sins, yet they implied that to be accepted by God we needed to keep the Old Testament commands about special days, the Sabbath, food regulations, and other Mosaic laws.

The world needs to know

Many who have been asked, have made comments that show how crucial it is to understand what it takes to be right with God, accepted by Him, and sure of heaven. You've probably heard these kinds of statements too:

- "I can't believe God will send a good non-Christian to hell and accept a bad Christian into heaven."
- "It sounds too easy to say that God forgives all our sins if we simply trust Jesus."
- "You have to be a member of the church and participate in all the rituals."
- "God doesn't care what you believe as long as you're sincere about it and try to be good."
- "My good deeds outweigh my bad ones."
- "I think I've been too bad to be forgiven."
- "God is too loving to send anyone to hell."
- "I'm saved by faith; how I live doesn't matter."
- "I don't want to believe in Jesus because I know I'll have to change the way I live."
- "God will grade us on a curve. After all, nobody's perfect."
- "People who just try to live like Jesus will probably be accepted into heaven."
- "It wouldn't be fair for God to allow a mass murderer to go to heaven."

You and I need to know

Perhaps one of these statements echoes your own thoughts as you've tried to sort through the issue of what it takes to gain God's approval and be accepted into heaven. It could be that you've never seen yourself as a person who needs to be saved from anything other than intolerant, Bible-toting religious types. Perhaps you are just the opposite, so overwhelmed by a sense of guilt over your past that you think you are a hopeless case. Perhaps you accepted Christ as your Savior when you were a child and you've been taking for granted all that Jesus has done for you. Or you may be thinking of your neighbors, friends, or those at work who need to hear the life-changing truth of how they can know that God accepts them now and forever.

In any case, I invite you to join me in looking closely at this crucial matter. No other topic has greater significance for the way we live right now and where we'll live eternally.

To better understand what's at stake, in the next few pages we will first focus on the issue that is at the heart of it all—justice. As we do, we'll look at justice from both the human and divine perspectives.

Chapter 14
When the Guilty Go Free

Crime is a way of life— and death—in so many parts of our world today. To make matters worse, justice can be elusive. Too often we hear of a criminal who escapes justice.

It makes us angry, doesn't it? It infuriates us to think of a rapist or child molester walking out of a courtroom with a smirk on his face because he outsmarted the system, or intimidated the victim or witnesses into silence. We're enraged when we hear of a criminal who goes free. It bothers us when the legal system seems more concerned about the rights of the criminal than of the victim.

Could God allow a mass murderer into heaven?

Is it possible that a person convicted of gruesome crimes could cry out to the Lord from his jail cell and be completely forgiven? This question should help us to focus on the key issue to be discussed in this chapter. The thought of a mass murderer sharing a mansion in heaven with you probably makes you shudder; it does me. But could it be possible?

"He who justifies the wicked, and he who condemns the just, both of them alike are
an abomination to the Lord."
Proverbs 17:15

To answer that question, let's think of another person—one of the two criminals crucified alongside Jesus. After hearing another dying criminal insult Jesus, he said, "'Don't you fear God, . . . since you are under the same sentence? We are punished justly, for we are getting what our deeds deserve. But this man has done nothing wrong.'

Then he said, 'Jesus, remember me when You come into Your kingdom.' Jesus answered him, 'I tell you the truth, today you will be with Me in paradise'" (Lk. 23:40-43NIV).

The repentant lawbreaker was forgiven by God just before he died. His guilt was erased; his criminal record wiped clean. Could it happen to a serial killer or child molester today?

How could it happen?

How could God be just in completely forgiving such a person? The apostle Paul learned firsthand how God could forgive a guilty person and still be an absolutely perfect and just Judge.

By his own admission, at one time Paul had been a self-righteous person who thought he deserved God's favor (see Phil. 3:4-6). He faithfully kept all the Jewish laws. And when he sensed a threat to the true worship of God by a group of zealous followers of a man they claimed was the promised Messiah, Paul did everything he could, even killing some and dragging others off to prison, to try to silence them (Acts 8:3, 22:4-5).

But one day Paul had a change of mind and heart. That's because he met Jesus, and Jesus helped Paul to see how wrong he was. As a result, Paul recognized his complete unworthiness of any favor from God and leaned upon His mercy. He believed that Jesus died in his place and made it possible for him to be right with God. In one of his letters, Paul called himself the worst of all sinners (1 Tim. 1:15), yet he firmly believed that he was headed for heaven because of Jesus.

Do we see ourselves in the picture?

We need to look beyond the examples of history to a very personal present-day dilemma. As we will see in the pages to follow, when judged by God's standards you and I are guilty of all sorts of crimes. We may have a hard time comprehending it, but we're really not any more qualified for heaven than a mass murderer. How, then, could we ever hope to sidestep justice and spend eternity in a place where only perfect people are admitted? How could God ever be right to say that imperfect, guilty people like you and me are free of the eternal consequences of our sin? Yet that's what the Bible tells us He does. If He

didn't, no one would ever be allowed inside the gates of heaven. We would all be sentenced to an eternity in hell.

Where are we going with this?

To find answers for our questions, we'll study the truths that are explained in the apostle Paul's letter to the followers of Christ in first-century Rome. In Paul's terms, the key word is justification. That term is one of many that we need to be familiar with as we read on.

So let's make sure we are speaking the same language before we address the reasons we can be accepted by God.

Following are some brief definitions we need to have in mind before we go any further.

Coming To Terms...

Faith: Dependence or reliance on someone (or something); trust or belief.

God's Grace: God's loving acts whereby He bestows undeserved favor.

God's Law: What God says is right or wrong, based on His perfect character qualities.

God's Mercy: The Lord's expression of withholding deserved punishment.

Guilt: God's declaration of wrongdoing.

Impute: To credit or transfer to the account of another.

Justification: God's once for- all declaration that a sinner is no longer under judgment but is the recipient of all the benefits of being right with Him because of what Jesus Christ has done.

Pardon: The action of a judge to withhold just punishment upon a lawbreaker; forgiveness.

Propitiation: The turning away of someone's anger and inflicting it upon a substitute.

Redemption: God's work of paying the penalty for our sin through the sacrificial death of Jesus.

Righteous: The condition of being approved by God; to be right in God's eyes.

Salvation: The act of God whereby He rescues sinners from eternal punishment.

Sanctification: The process whereby a follower of Christ becomes more and more like Him.

Sin: A violation of God's laws; failing to measure up to His standards of what is right; disobedience.

How Can We Be Accepted By God?

What happens when you get struck by lightning—twice? Martin Luther knew. The first time was during his studies as a law student. On a steamy summer evening in July, 1505, as he was walking outside, a lightning bolt hit so close to him that it knocked him to the ground. In terror he vowed to become a monk. Within a month he quit his legal studies and checked into a monastery.

But Luther's soul was restless. The more he knew about God, the more inadequate he felt. He tried fasting, giving himself to prayer, and spending hours in confession. After years of frustration, depression, and struggling with an overwhelming sense of guilt and unworthiness to be accepted by God, Luther was "struck by lightning" again—the lightning of God's truth.

In the early 1500s, Luther created quite a stir when he parted company with the established church of his day. Why did he hammer 95 theses on the door of a Wittenburg church? Luther had discovered a liberating, life-changing, and eternally significant truth. Having tried desperately many times to prove to God that he was good enough to deserve His favor, Luther's eyes were opened. He Luther's soul was restless. The more he knew about God, the more inadequate he felt. finally understood how God could call a bad person good—worthy to be called a child of God, worthy to enter heaven.

While he was reading the New Testament book of Romans, it was as if his soul was struck by lightning. The flash of God-given insight gave him everything he had been searching for—and more.

Because the book of Romans so clearly explains the truth of justification, we will be taking a close look at the same verses that changed Luther's life and the course of church history.

If you are studying this book by yourself or with a group, and you would like to do some firsthand discovery, I would encourage you to take time to read the designated parts of Romans listed below. As you read, search for answers to the key questions that are listed.

No Excuses

In this section we will look at Romans 1:1–3:20. Some key questions are:

1. Why do people choose to disobey God?
2. Why are our excuses groundless?
3. How does God express His kindness?
4. What will happen to spiritual rebels?
5. Who can measure up to God's standards?
6. What good is God's law?

What makes God angry?

Some people would rather not think about this possibility. They would like to imagine that God is so loving that He could never get mad at anyone. The first chapters of Romans, however, let us know upfront that because sin makes God furious we need to be justified. Hell is not simply a myth or a preacher's scare tactic. It is a very real destination for all who refuse to turn from their self-serving ways to the Lord Jesus.

In Romans 1:16-18 the apostle wrote:

I am not ashamed of the gospel of Christ, for it is the power of God to salvation for everyone who believes, for the Jew first and also for the Greek. For in it the righteousness of God is revealed from faith to faith; as it is written, "The just shall live by faith." For the wrath of God is revealed from heaven against all ungodliness and unrighteousness of men, who suppress the truth in unrighteousness.

Those verses present the stark contrast between the person who humbly expresses faith in Christ and the person who deliberately pushes away and buries the truth of what God says. The heart of sin is the attitude that we cannot trust God to give us what is best for us. It is selfish arrogance that leads us to reject God's rules and establish our own code of ethics grounded only in our fickle self-centeredness. That is why the statement is true that very few people reject Christ for intellectual reasons; most people reject Him because they do not want to change their way of life.

Why doesn't God accept excuses?

Paul told us that the basic knowledge of God's existence and His power is an obvious fact of life. The universe around us points to an all-wise, all-powerful Creator. Because of that, none of us can say that God has left us in the dark. What may be known of God is manifest in them, for God has shown it to them. For since the creation of the world His invisible attributes are clearly seen, being understood by the things that are made, even His eternal power and Godhead, so that they are without excuse (vv.19-20).

Instead of worshiping the Creator, people bowed before objects of God's creation (v.23).

In addition, the human conscience is a built-in mirror of God's laws (2:15). True, this inner awareness of what is right and wrong can be ignored and deadened (1 Tim. 4:2), but it is one more reason that none of us will have an excuse when we stand before God on judgment day (Rom. 2:16).

Was Paul talking about me?

To make his point so clear that we couldn't miss it, Paul described two specific types of people who have no legitimate defense for their sin. All of us fit into one of these categories.

The pleasure-seeker (1:26-32). Also known as a hedonist, this type of person is controlled by a thirsty lust for personal gratification. Paul lists several characteristics of pleasure seekers: sexual promiscuity, homosexuality, greed, envy, murder, strife, deceit, malice, gossip, slander, hatred of God, violence, arrogance, disobedience to parents. They are undiscerning, untrustworthy, unloving, unforgiving, unmerciful, approving of evil.

The self-righteous (2:1–3:8). This type of person would never think of himself as a pleasure seeking pagan. In fact, he's appalled at the blatant godlessness of many people in society. He acknowledges God's existence and the reality of being accountable to Him. But he has a problem—he's a hypocrite. He's quick to point out the sins of others but slow to recognize the magnitude of his own violations of God's laws. Blind to his own faults, he readily sees that other people are headed for a terrible day of judgment, but he doesn't realize that he faces the same judgment.

The apostle Paul explained that being "religious" and being part of a family with a long history of religious activities do not make a person right with God. Paul specifically debunked the notion that being born a Jew made a person acceptable to God and exempt from judgment. This is a truth every religious person needs to think about. Merely having godly parents, attending church, giving money to missions, or serving in the various programs of the church do not make us acceptable to God. Scientists will never find a human gene for godliness.

Why can't our good deeds outweigh our bad ones and make God happy with us?

In case we missed it before, Paul said it one more time and so directly that we can't escape the conclusion: No one can ever do enough good to counterbalance the terrible weight of even one sin. Paul wrote: What then? Are we better than they? Not at all. For we have previously charged both Jews and Greeks that they are all under sin. As it is written: "There is none righteous, no, not one; there is none who understands; there is none who seeks after God. They have all turned aside; they have together become unprofitable; there is none who does good, no, not one." "Their throat is an open tomb; with their tongues they have practiced deceit"; "the poison of asps is under their lips"; "whose mouth is full of cursing and bitterness." "Their feet are swift to shed blood; destruction and misery are in their ways; and the way of peace they have not known." "There is no fear of God before their eyes." Now we know that whatever the law says, it says to those who are under the law, that every mouth may be stopped, and all the world may become guilty before God. Therefore by the deeds of the law no flesh will be justified in His sight, for by the law is the knowledge of sin (3:9-20).

The conclusion: We all stand before God "guilty as charged." Every one of us has in some way violated God's law. Merely trying to do good does not erase the bad. In God's courtroom, where He is the Lawmaker, Judge, and Jury, we stand totally helpless, without one shred of legitimate evidence as to why He should not "throw the book" at us.

So what should we do? Give up? No. Paul's purpose in bringing us to the end of ourselves is to show us how much we need Christ to come to our rescue. In the next part of Romans we will see how God can be a just Judge and yet free us from the penalty of our sin.

Chapter 15
One Substitution

In this section we will look at Romans 3:21–4:25 and 9:1–11:36.

Some key questions are:

1. How can we be right with God?
2. Who took our punishment? Why?
3. Why is so much said about Abraham?
4. Why can't we accuse God of being unjust?
5. Why can't we take pride in our faith?

How can God say we're right when we're wrong?

Romans 3:21-26 is crucial to our understanding of this issue. But now the righteousness of God apart from the law is revealed, being witnessed by the Law and the Prophets, even the righteousness of God, through faith in Jesus Christ, to all and on all who believe. For there is no difference; for all have sinned and fall short of the glory of God, being justified freely by His grace through the redemption that is in Christ Jesus, whom God set forth as a propitiation by His blood, through faith, to demonstrate His righteousness, because in His forbearance God had passed over the sins that were previously committed, to demonstrate at the present time His righteousness, that He might be just and the justifier of the one who has faith in Jesus.

Let's summarize the key points of these verses:

• God graciously has taken the initiative to provide a way for us to be right with Him.

• No one is able to keep His laws.

• Putting our trust in Christ, rather than in trying to be good, makes us right with God.

• Jesus' sacrificial death paid the penalty we deserved. As our substitute, He experienced the wrath of God against sin.

• God's justice is satisfied and we are declared right with Him because of what Jesus did for us, not because of what we do for ourselves.

- God withheld ultimate judgment on sin until Christ became our substitute.
- As Judge, God says we are in the wrong; as the Justifier, He declares that we are now in the right.

What does justification mean for us?

It means that our guilt is gone and Christ's righteousness has been given to us. God can call bad people good because Jesus gave Himself as our substitute in His death and in His life. So when God looks at us, He sees Jesus Christ. Let's go back to the definition given earlier in this chapter: "Justification is God's once-for-all declaration that a sinner is no longer under judgment but is the recipient of all the benefits of being right with Him because of what Jesus Christ has done."

Bible teacher Warren Wiersbe states, "Justification is the act of God whereby He declares the believing sinner righteous in Christ on the basis of the finished work of Christ on the cross" (Be Right, p.35).

Pastor and author Charles Swindoll writes, "Justification is God's merciful act, whereby He declares righteous the believing sinner while he is still in his sinning state.

He sees us in our need, wallowing around in the swamp of our sin. He sees us looking to Jesus Christ and trusting Him completely by faith, to cleanse us from our sin. And though we come to Him with all of our needs and in all of our darkness, God says to us, 'Declared righteous! Forgiven! Pardoned!'" (Growing Deep In The Christian Life, p.238).

Does it mean "just as if I'd never sinned"?

This has been a popular definition used often in Sunday school classes. It has some merit to it, but it may also give the wrong impression.

On the positive side, this definition is in line with what Paul said in Romans about being declared right with God. Justification means that God applies to our account all the perfect goodness of Christ. The stigma of guilt is gone. But it certainly cannot be true that we were innocent of all charges—we did sin. Nor does it mean that a huge price did not have to be paid to free us from the guilt of our sins. The truth is, we stand before God as forgiven sinners whose deserved punishment was taken by our substitute, the Lord Jesus Christ.

Why did Paul write an entire chapter about Abraham?

What can we learn about justification from a man who lived 2,000 years before Christ?

Paul devoted a whole chapter to Abraham because so many of the people to whom Paul was writing were Jews. And of course all Jews trace their ancestry back to Abraham. From his own personal experience, Paul knew the danger of trusting in his connection to Abraham genetically and through the physical mark of circumcision rather than establishing a vital faith relationship with God. Paul and his fellow Jews had been trying to be right with God by keeping the laws God communicated to Moses. But they had become deluded into thinking that they were on good terms with God through their attempts at keeping the Law. They were trusting in themselves rather than God's mercy and grace to be revealed in the promised Messiah.

Paul quoted from Genesis 15:6 when he wrote, "For what does the Scripture say? 'Abraham believed God, and it was accounted to him for righteousness'" (4:3). Paul then said, "Now to him who works, the wages are not counted as grace but as debt. But to him who does not work but believes on Him who justifies the ungodly, his faith is accounted for righteousness, just as David also describes the blessedness of the man to whom God imputes righteousness apart from works" (vv.4-6).

The key point of the chapter is this: God declared Abraham to be righteous before Abraham submitted to the physical rite of circumcision. Abraham was not declared right because he did something to earn it but because he simply trusted God to do what He said He would do.

Isn't this too easy?

Shouldn't we have to do something? Many have a hard time with the concept of justification. It seems too easy, so undemanding of them. They would like to think that either by doing a lot of humanitarian service or by devoting themselves to prayer and fasting or other rituals that they can somehow become worthy of salvation. The Bible says, however, that such efforts are absolutely worthless to earn salvation.

Look at what the apostle Paul wrote to the Philippians. After listing all of the "religious" pre-conversion activities by which he had sought God's favor, Paul said: What things were gain to me, these I have counted loss for Christ. Yet indeed I also count all things loss for the excellence of the knowledge of Christ Jesus my Lord, for whom I have suffered the loss of all things, and count them as rubbish, that I may gain Christ and be found in Him, not having my own righteousness, which is from the law, but that which is through faith in Christ, the righteousness which is from God by faith (3:7-9).

And in his letter to a group of believers in Ephesus, Paul emphasized that salvation is the "gift of God"—the result of His work, not our own works. For by grace you have been saved through faith, and that not of yourselves; it is the gift of God, not of works, lest anyone should boast. For we are His workmanship, created in Christ Jesus for good works, which

God prepared beforehand that we should walk in them (2:8-10).

How did Martin Luther respond to this truth?

We mentioned earlier how the truth of justification by faith revolutionized Luther's thinking. In his own words, here is how it happened: I greatly longed to understand Paul's epistle to the Romans and nothing stood in the way but that one expression, "the justice of God," because I took it to mean that justice whereby God is just and deals justly in punishing the unjust. My situation was that, although an impeccable monk, I stood before God as a sinner troubled in conscience, and I had no confidence that my merit would assuage Him. Therefore I did not love a just and angry God, but rather hated and murmured against Him. Yet I clung to the dear Paul and had a great yearning to know what he meant. Night and day I pondered until I saw the connection between the justice of God and the statement that "the just shall live by faith." Then I grasped that the justice of God is that righteousness by which through grace and sheer mercy God justifies us through faith. Thereupon I felt myself to be reborn and to have gone through open doors into paradise. The whole of Scripture took on a new meaning, and whereas before the "justice of God" had filled me with hate, now it became to me inexpressibly sweet in greater love. This passage of Paul became to me a gate of heaven (Quoted by church historian Roland Bainton in his biography of Luther, Here I Stand).

Does this seem unjust to you?

In Romans 9–11 Paul answered an objection he anticipated from his readers. Because salvation is initiated by God and justification is a sovereign work of God in the lives of people He chooses to rescue, some people may accuse God of being unfair in justifying some and not others.

Paul's whole argument, however, up to this point in Romans, was that salvation is totally undeserved, unearned, and unrelated to any attempts at righteousness by any man or woman. Paul said, "It does not . . . depend on man's desire or effort, but on God's mercy" (9:16 NIV). This is a hard truth for many people to accept because it deflates our pride—we have absolutely nothing to offer to God. All we can do is accept by faith what He has offered to us.

Where did the Jews go wrong? Paul said that Israel pursued righteousness and failed "because they did not seek it by faith, but as it were, by the works of the law. . . . For they being ignorant of God's righteousness, and seeking to establish their own righteousness, have not submitted to the righteousness of God" (9:32; 10:3).

In contrast, the offer of salvation is now open to all who will accept it by faith as a gift. If you confess with your mouth the Lord Jesus and believe in your heart that God has raised

Him from the dead, you will be saved. For with the heart one believes unto righteousness, and with the mouth confession is made unto salvation. For the Scripture says, "Whoever believes on Him will not be put to shame." For there is no distinction between Jew and Greek, for the same Lord over all is rich to all who call upon Him. For "whoever calls on the name of the Lord shall be saved" (10:9-13).

Does James contradict Paul's teaching of justification by faith?

The author of the short letter that bears his name is believed to be the oldest half-brother of Jesus. After some years of disbelief (Jn. 7:2-5), James too accepted the truth that Jesus was the Savior, and James became a leader in the early church (Acts 12:17; 15:13), and he is even mentioned favorably by Paul (Gal. 1:19; 2:9).

So why does it seem to some people that James (whose letter was written before Romans) and Paul don't agree on this most basic issue of salvation? The problem arises if we take what James said out of the broader context of the point he was trying to make. James wrote: What does it profit, my brethren, if someone says he has faith but does not have works? Can faith save him? (Jas. 2:14). James then gave a practical example of responding to a person who needs food and clothes. It is worthless, he argued, to utter a word of blessing and not give food or clothing. He continued: Thus also faith by itself, if it does not have works, is dead. But someone will say, "You have faith, and I have works." Show me your faith without your works, and I will show you my faith by my works (Jas. 2:14,17-18). Then James, like Paul, cited the example of Abraham to prove his point. He wrote: Was not Abraham our father justified by works when he offered Isaac his son on the altar? Do you see that faith was working together with his works, and by works faith was made perfect? And the Scripture was fulfilled which says, "Abraham believed God, and it was accounted to him for righteousness." . . . You see then that a man is justified by works, and not by faith only (vv.21-24). What would Paul have said in response? He would have agreed wholeheartedly because he and James were addressing two related but different aspects of justification. Paul spoke of God's action of justification by which He declares a person right with Him at the moment that person puts trust in Jesus as Savior. James wrote of the visible evidence of justification that occurs in a person's new way of life. In the first sense, we are declared righteous in God's eyes. In the second sense, we are declared righteous in the eyes of people.

J. Ronald Blue, in The Bible Knowledge Commentary, writes, "Together Paul and James give the full dimension of faith. Paul wrote about inner saving faith from God's perspective. James wrote about outward serving faith from man's perspective. The true seed of saving faith is verified by the tangible fruit of serving faith. James' point is that biblical faith works" (p.816).

The French reformer John Calvin (1509-1564) explained the statements of James this way: As Paul contends that men are justified without the aid of good works, so James will not allow any to be regarded as justified who are destitute of good works. Due attention to the scope will thus disentangle every doubt; for the error of our opponents lies chiefly in this, that they think James is defining the mode of justification, whereas his only object is to destroy the depraved security of those who vainly pretended faith as an excuse for their contempt of good works. Therefore, let them twist the words of James as they may, they will never extract out of them more than the two propositions: That an empty phantom of faith does not justify, and that the believer, not contented with such an imagination, manifests his justification by good works (John Calvin, Institutes Of The Christian Religion, translated by Henry Beveridge).

As we will see, the apostle Paul also proclaimed strongly that a person who has genuine faith in Christ will exhibit a new way of life, a life consistent with a claim to have been declared right with God.

Chapter 16
Many Results

In this section we will look at Romans 5–8 and 12–16. Some key questions are:
1. What are the results of justification?
2. Why should believers take sin seriously?
3. Why should we work hard to be good?
4. How does God help us to be good?
5. How do forgiven people live?

What difference does justification make?

Marriage is a good analogy of the relationship between a legal pronouncement and the practical outworking of it. The marriage ceremony, like justification, is a declaration that a new relationship has been entered. A man and woman, formerly unrelated, enter a legal contract that should change their lives. Suddenly, they share possessions, they share the same dwelling, and they look to the future as a time when their relationship will grow closer and richer. Legally, marriage changes so much. On the other hand, a pronouncement of marriage doesn't make the man and woman perfect partners in life. They have to stop thinking and living like single persons and begin to think and live like married persons. So too, once we have been legally justified by God, we have established a relationship that needs to be cultivated.

The marriage analogy can be taken only so far because marriages don't always last. But when God justifies us and brings us into a new relationship with Him, He never divorces us. Nothing can ever separate us from Christ's love (Rom. 8:38-39). We may fail Him repeatedly, but He is committed to make the relationship last forever, eventually making it perfect (vv.29-30). Remember, justification is based on what God has done, not on our works.

What are the practical benefits of justification?

As we indicated in the previous section, Paul would have agreed wholeheartedly with James that justification is not the end of the story. Just as a farmer expects an apple tree to produce fruit, so God is committed to working in a justified person's life to bring about more and more fruit of right behavior. A person who is justified does not automatically become perfect and cease to be a sinner in need of great improvement.

In Romans 5–8, Paul goes to great lengths to show the benefits of being right with God. Here is a partial listing. We have:

- peace with God (5:1).
- hope that God will finish what He started in us (v.2).
- a sense of God's love through the Holy Spirit who now lives within (v.5).
- assurance that we will not face God's wrath; we have been reconciled to Him (vv.9-11).
- eternal life (v.21).
- the ability to live a new way of life (6:4).
- the hope of a future resurrection (v.5).
- freedom from sin's tyranny; the opportunity to live as God's servants (vv.6-23).
- an obligation to depend on the Spirit of God and not measure our spirituality by our ability to keep rules (7:1-6).

- a struggle with sin that we will ultimately win through Jesus Christ (vv.7-25).
- the help and power of the Holy Spirit to enable us to do what is right (8:1-11).
- a closeness to God; we can now call Him Father (vv.15-16).
- a new status as heirs of God and co-heirs of Christ's glory (v.17).
- hope of one day receiving the full benefits of being children of God (vv.23-25).
- the Spirit's help when we pray (vv.26-27).
- the certain hope that we will one day be as perfect as Christ (vv.28-31).
- the reassurance that nothing can divorce us from our relationship with God (vv.31-39).

What are we supposed to do?

Now that we have been given so much as a result of being justified, how does God expect us to work on our side of the relationship? Chapters 12–16 of Romans give us many down-to-earth instructions on how we are to live.

The difference between who we are as justified sinners and the process of becoming more like Christ as His followers is sometimes referred to by the terms standing and state (or position and practice). Our official, God-declared and once-for-all standing as believers in Christ is that we are justified, seen by God as possessing the righteousness of Christ. Our state is our present-day level of spiritual maturity as Christ-followers. It refers to our level of dependence on Christ, our commitment to His ways, the practical day-to-day outworking of our faith in making choices that God says are right.

What Paul describes in Romans 12–16 relates to that expression of faith in everyday life. We are to:

• offer our bodies to the Lord (12:1).

• resist the pressures of the world to conform to sinful thoughts and actions, and instead allow God to transform our minds (v.2).

• serve other believers with our God-given abilities (vv.3-8).

• love sincerely (v.9).

• hate evil, cling to the good (v.9).

• serve the good of others (v.10).

• live joyfully, patiently in trouble, faithfully in prayer (v.12).

• be charitable and hospitable (v.13).

• not be vengeful (vv.14,17).

• show empathy (v.15).

• avoid prejudice (v.16).

• do what produces peace and counters evil with good (vv.17-21).

- submit to authorities and the law (13:1-7).
- love others (vv.8-11).
- behave decently, not even thinking about giving in to temptation (vv.12-14).
- do all we can to get along with other believers and strengthen their faith (14:1–15:13).
- beware of false teachers (16:17-19).

That may seem like a long list, but there are many more exhortations in the Bible. As you read the New Testament, you will find time and time again that Christ and His apostles urged believers to put their faith into practice.

Earlier we referred to Ephesians 2:8-10. Let's take one more look at verse 10, for it has something significant to say to us in this current discussion: "For we are His workmanship, created in Christ Jesus for good works, which God prepared beforehand that we should walk in them." Immediately after making the point that we are saved by faith and not by works, Paul quickly reminded his readers that we are "created in Christ Jesus" for the very purpose of doing good works. In fact, it is all part of God's plan from the very beginning: "God prepared beforehand that we should walk in them." It couldn't be said more clearly or forcefully than that.

So why do so many people think they need to earn their own salvation?

Could it be a matter of pride? It is very humbling to have to admit that we are totally unworthy of God's mercy and grace. As we saw in Part 1: No Excuses, nobody has anything to brag about before God. That strikes at the very core of our problem. Ever since Adam and Eve took a bite out of the forbidden fruit, we as members of the human race have a tendency to think we know better than God what is best for us. We have an overblown sense of our importance, our abilities, and our goodness. But God shatters all that arrogance with a call for humble repentance and an acceptance of salvation, in the way a starving beggar would accept a morsel of food.

Or perhaps someone thinks he has been so bad that God could never consider him acceptable. God says we're all deserving of hell. And as far as God is concerned, no sin (except total rejection of Him) is too bad to be forgiven. Remember the apostle Paul? Because of his self-righteousness and his persecution of Christians before his conversion, he considered himself the worst of sinners, yet he was absolutely sure that God had accepted him.

What about the verses in the Bible that make it sound as if we are saved by works?

Those verses that at first reading seem to imply that our salvation is based on a judgment of our actions must be taken in the total context of what Christ and the apostles taught.

James Montgomery Boice speaks to this issue in his book Foundations Of The Christian Faith. After listing several of Christ's parables and teachings that might be taken as promoting salvation by works, Boice writes, "These stories and other sayings of Jesus seem to teach that people are saved on the basis of their perseverance, foresight, enterprise, or charity. But this problem vanishes when we realize that Jesus is not contradicting but rather is showing the consequences of what it means genuinely to believe on Him as Savior" (pp.429-430).

What do your works say about you?

When people look at you and me, do they see evidence that God has done His work in our lives? Do they see the fruit of justification and God's regenerating work? (Jn. 3). Although it's true that God's justification comes to all who will accept it by trusting Christ, no one should make the mistake of thinking that he can come to Christ for salvation while retaining his old way of life. True faith produces the fruit of repentance and devotion to Christ. It's that simple.

Have you, like Martin Luther, been "struck by lightning" as you've read through Romans? If so, rejoice in what Christ has done for you and share your newfound discovery with others.

On Trial

If you were suddenly transported into the presence of God and you heard a prosecuting attorney listing all the reasons you should be sent to hell, how would you plead? Guilty or not guilty?

The apostle Paul said, "For all have sinned and fall short of the glory of God" (Rom. 3:23). That makes us guilty as charged.

What is the penalty for our sin? "The wages of sin is death, but the gift of God is eternal life in Christ Jesus our Lord" (Rom. 6:23).

What could we say in our defense? "God demonstrates His own love toward us, in that while we were still sinners, Christ died for us" (Rom. 5:8).

Because Jesus became our substitute, the penalty has been paid. But we must accept His forgiveness as a gift. The only requirement is that we recognize our need and accept His offer.

"If you confess with your mouth the Lord Jesus and believe in your heart that God has raised Him from the dead, you will be saved. . . . For 'whoever calls on the name of the Lord shall be saved'" (Rom. 10:9,13).

If you haven't done so before, tell Jesus that you believe He died as your substitute and accept the free and undeserved gift of forgiveness. That's the only way to be right about your wrong, to be accepted by God, and to be sure of heaven.

Selected Bibliography

Aland, Kurt. *The Greek New Testament with Dictionary.* Edmonds: United Bible Society 1966

Anders, Max. *30 Days to Understanding the Bible.* Dallas: Word 1988

_____. *30 Days to Understanding the Christian Life in 15 Minutes a Day!* Nashville: Nelson 1990

_____. *30 Days to Understanding What Christians Believe.* Nashville: Thomas Nelson 1994

_____. *New Christian's Handbook.* Nashville: Nelson 1999

Anderson, Ken. *Where to Find it in the Bible.* Nashville: Nelson 1996

Barnes, Peter. *Out of Darkness into Light.* San Diego: Equippers 1984

_____. *The Truth about Jesus and the Trinity.* San Diego: Equipper's 1989

Blomberg, Craig. *1 Corinthians.* Grand Rapids: Zondervan 1995

Booth, A. E. *The Course of Time from Eternity to Eternity.* Neptune: Loizeaux Brothers

Braga, James. *How to Study the Bible.* Portland: Multnomah 1982

Brown, Francis and et al. *The Brown-Driver-Briggs Hebrew and English Lexicon.* Peabody: Hendrickson 1999

Bruce, A. B. *The Training of the Twelve.* Grand Rapids: Kregel 1971

Bullinger, E. W. *Figures of Speech Used in the Bible.* Grand Rapids: Baker 1968

Burton, Sam Westman. *Disciple Mentoring.* Pasadena: William Carey 2000

Cairns, Earle E. *Christianity through the Centuries.* Grand Rapids: Zondervan 1954

Chafer, Lewis Sperry. *Grace.* Grand Rapids: Kregel 1922

_____. *He that is Spiritual.* Grand Rapids: Zondervan 1918

_____. *Salvation.* Grand Rapids: Kregel 1991

_____. *Systematic Theology 1- 8 set.* Kregel

Cole, R. Alan. *Galatians.* Grand Rapids: IVP / Eerdmans 1965

Couch, Mal. *The Fundamentals for the Twenty-First Century.* Grand Rapids: Kregel 2000

Cox, Steven. *Essentials of New Testament Greek - A Student's Guide.* Broadman & Holman

Dana, H. E. and Julius R. Mantey. *A Manual Grammar of the Greek New Testament.* Upper Saddle River: Prentice Hall 1927

Elliger, K. *Biblia Hebraica – Stuttgartensia.* Deutsche Biblegesellschaft 1969

Elwell, Walter A. *Evangelical Dictionary of Theology.* Cumbria: Baker 1984

Enns, Paul. *The Moody Handbook of Theology.* Chicago: Moody 1989

Evans, Tony. *America's Only Hope.* Chicago: Moody 1990

_____. *Our God is Awesome.* Chicago: Moody 1994

Foulkes, Francis. *Ephesians.* Grand Rapids: IVP / Eerdmans 1963

Halley, Henry H. *Halley's Bible Handbook.* Grand Rapids: Zondervan 1927

Hastings, James - Ed. *Hastings' Dictionary of the Bible.* New York: Hendrickson 1909

Hodges, C. Zane. *The Greek New Testament according to the Majority Text.* Nashville: Nelson 1985

Hoekema, Anthony A. *Created in God's Image.* Grand Rapids: Eerdmans 1986

_____. *Saved by Grace.* Grand Rapids: Eerdmans 1989

House, H. Wayne - Ed. *Chronological and Background Charts of the New Testament.* Grand Rapids: Zondervan 1981

_____. and Kenneth M. Durharn. *Living Wisely in a Foolish World.* Grand Rapids: Kregel 1992

Hughes, R. Kent. *Disciplines of a Godly Man.* Wheaton: Crossway 1991

Hutchcraft, Ron. *The Battle for a Generation.* Chicago: Moody 1996

Jensen, Irving L. *Jensen's Survey of the New Testament.* Chicago: Moody 1981

_____. *Jensen's Survey of the Old Testament.* Chicago: Moody 1978

Kent, Homer A. *A Heart Opened Wide - Studies in 2 Corinthians.* Winona Lake: BMH Books 1982

_____. *Faith that Works.* Winona Lake: BMH Books 1986

_____. *Light in the Darkness.* Winona Lake: BMH Books 1974

_____. *The Epistle to the Hebrews.* Winona Lake: BMH Books 1972

_____. *The Freedom of God's Sons.* Winona Lake: BMH Books 1976

_____. *The Pastoral Epistles (1 & 2 Timothy and Titus). Winona Lake:* BMH Books 1986

_____. *Treasures of Wisdom.* Winona Lake: BMH Books 1978

Kubo, Sakae. *A Reader's Greek-English Lexicon of the New Testament.* Zondervan

Little, Paul. *How to Give Away Your Faith.* Downers Grove: IVP 1966

MacArthur, John F. and Wayne A. Mack. *Ashamed of the Gospel.* Wheaton: Crossway 1993

_____. *Our Sufficiency in Christ.* Dallas: Word Publishing 1991.

McClain, Alva J. *Romans.* Winona Lake: BMH Books 1973

_____. *The Greatness of the Kingdom.* BMH Books

McDowell, Josh. *A Ready Defense.* Nashville: Nelson 1993

McDowell, Josh. *Evidence that Demands a Verdict.* Nashville: Nelson 1975

McGee, J. Vernon. *The Best of J. Vernon McGee. Volume 1.* Nashville: Thomas Nelson 1988.

_____. *Thru the Bible with J. Vernon McGee.* Nashville: Thomas Nelson Publishers 1981.

_____. *Jesus: Centerpiece of Scripture.* Nashville: Thomas Nelson publishers 1995.

Morris, Leon. *1 & 2 Thessalonians.* Grand Rapids: IVP / Eerdmans 1956

Perschbacher, Wesley J. *The New Analytical Greek Lexicon.* Peabody: Hendrickson 1990

Radmacher, Earl and et al - Eds. *New Illustrated Bible Commentary.* Nashville: Nelson 1999

Robertson, Archibald. *Word Pictures in the New Testament Set 1 – 6.* Broadman

Ryrie, Charles C. *Balancing the Christian Life.* Chicago: Moody 1969

_____. *Basic Theology.* Chicago: Moody 1986

_____. *So Great Salvation.* Chicago: Moody 1997

_____. *The Holy Spirit.* Chicago: Moody 1965

Saucy, Robert L. *The Church in God's Program.* Chicago: Moody 1972

Strong, James. *The New Strong's Exhaustive Concordance of the Bible*. Nashville: Nelson 1964

Spurgeon, C.H. *The Life and Work of Our Lord* Vol 1-3. Grand Rapids: Baker Books 1904

Summers, Ray. *Essentials of New Testament Greek*. Nashville: Broadman & Holman 1995

Tenney, Merrill C. *Galatians*. Grand Rapids: Eerdmans 1950

Unger, Merrill F. *The New Unger's Bible Dictionary*. Moody

Vine, W. E. *Vine's Complete Expository Dictionary*. Nashville: Nelson 1984

Wallace, Daniel B. *Greek Grammar Beyond the Basics*. Grand Rapids: Zondervan 1996

Walvoord, John F. and Roy B. Zuck. *The Bible Knowledge Commentary (New Testament)*. Colorado Springs: Victor 1983

_____. *Jesus Christ Our Lord*. Chicago: Moody 1969

_____. *The Holy Spirit*. Grand Rapids: Zondervan 1954

_____. *The Revelation of Jesus Christ*. Chicago: Moody 1966

Wiersbe, Warren W. *The Bible Exposition Commentary*. Colorado Springs: Victor 1989

_____. *Wiersbe's Expository Outlines on the New Testament*. Colorado Springs:

_____. *Wiersbe's Expository Outlines on the Old Testament*. Colorado Springs: Victor 1993

Wigram, George V. and Ralph D. Winter. *The Word Study New Testament and Concordance.* Wheaton: Wheaton 1972

Wilberforce, William. *A Practical View of Christianity* Peabody: Hendrickson 1996

Wilkinson, Bruce and Kenneth Boa. *Talk thru the Bible.* Nashville: Nelson 1983

Youngblood, Ronald F., General Editor; F.F. Bruce and R.K. Harrison, Consulting Editors. *Nelson's New Illustrated Bible Dictionary.* Nashville, TN: Thomas Nelson 1995.

Zodhiates, Spiros. *The Complete Word Study Dictionary of the New Testament.* Chattanooga: AMG Publishers 1992

Zuck, Roy B. - Ed. *A Biblical Theology of the New Testament.* Chicago: Moody 1994

_____. - Ed. *A Biblical Theology of the Old Testament.* Chicago: Moody 1991

_____. *Basic Bible Interpretation.* Colorado Springs: Victor 1991

_____. The Bible Knowledge Commentary 2 Vol. Set. Colorado Springs: Victor 1983

Also Available:

Simple Theology:
Theology for the Rest of Us
Clay A. Kahler Ph.D.

This survey of theology is suited for every believer, regardless of previous knowledge or spiritual maturity. Dr. Kahler presents theological truths in a way that is easy to understand and will spur the reader on to further study.

ISBN: 1579108873

Available from Christian bookstores and online book sellers nationwide.

Against Protestant Popes:
An Exegetical Study of 1 Peter 5:1-4 (Paperback)
Clay A. Kahler Ph.D.

A BIBLICAL LOOK at God's awesome call to be a shepherd to His flock. This exegetical look at Peter's admonition to "fellow Shepherds" will cause those in ministry to look very hard at their own model of ministry. Packed full of Biblical insights, this is a must read for all of those in or considering the ministry.

ISBN: 1597521493

Available from Christian bookstores and online book sellers nationwide.

Torn Asunder:
A Biblical Look at Divorce and Remarriage (Paperback)
Dr. Clay A. Kahler

In *Torn Asunder: A Biblical Look at Divorce and Remarriage* Dr. Kahler tackles one of today's most controversial topics. When discussing divorce and remarriage passions run deep. That is why this book is so important. Dr. Kahler leads the reader through a Biblical exploration seeking God's instruction, dispelling myths and tackling tradition. No matter your feelings on the subject, this book will help you discover God's heart concerning those who have been hurt and those currently suffering.

ISBN: 1597528072

Available from Christian bookstores and online book sellers nationwide.

www.ingramcontent.com/pod-product-compliance
Lightning Source LLC
Chambersburg PA
CBHW070922180426
43192CB00037B/1678